THE MAN WHO TRANSFORMED THE WORLD

James Watt

Born: January 19, 1736
Died: August 19, 1819

Even as a child, James Watt had an inventive turn of mind and was fascinated by everything mechanical. As an instrument maker he acquired dexterity and skill, and while employed by the University of Glasgow he became intrigued by the enormous possibilities of steam power. He envisioned a steam engine that would free man from the burden of hand operations, but was too poor to undertake long years of experimentation. When he met Matthew Boulton who was willing to finance his project, he realized his dream but had to fight ignorance, ridicule and resistance to new ideas. His condensing steam engine brought about the Industrial Revolution, thus changing the social and economic structures of the world.

Books by William D. Crane

CANCER, COCAINE AND COURAGE
   The Story of Dr. William Halsted
      (with Arthur J. Beckhard)

THE DISCOVERER OF OXYGEN
   Joseph Priestley

THE MAN WHO TRANSFORMED THE WORLD
   James Watt

THE MAN WHO TRANSFORMED THE WORLD

James Watt

by **William D. Crane**

JULIAN MESSNER, INC. · NEW YORK

Published by Julian Messner, Inc.
8 West 40th Street, New York 18

Published simultaneously in Canada
by The Copp Clark Publishing Co. Limited

© Copyright 1963 by William D. Crane

Printed in the United States of America
Library of Congress Catalog Card No. 63-16785

To Peg

Soon shall thy arm, unconquered steam, afar
Drag the slow barge, or drive the rapid car
Or on wide, wavering wings expanded bear
The flying chariot through the field of air.

Erasmus Darwin, 1780

THE MAN WHO
TRANSFORMED
THE WORLD

James Watt

ONE

THE YEAR WAS 1742. THE PLACE WAS THE LITTLE TOWN of Greenock on the west coast of Scotland. The children of the local public school were noisily enjoying a morning recess from their studies, running and skipping about in all directions. Suddenly the noise was stilled, and like a flock of birds the boys all wheeled toward one corner of the playfield. There were rather muffled cries of "What's up?" "Who is it?" as they crowded around a little boy sitting on the ground with his head bowed in his hands.

"It's Jamie Watt," one boy told another, and the report soon reached the outer edge of the crowd. A teacher pushed his way through and carried the little six-year-old boy into the school. After a few minutes' rest Jamie sat up and smiled rather weakly. "It's my head," he said, "but it's all right now." By this time his mother had been sent for, and she patted his hand encouragingly. "I'll take you home, Jamie," she told him, and she carried him home in spite of his urgent protests that he could walk. Agnes Muirhead Watt had lost her first three children, her fifth one, John, aged three, was quite healthy. This fourth one, little Jamie, was not going to be taken from her. She was going to see to that.

Consultations with a doctor, long words that Jamie didn't understand, and a great deal of thumping on his chest all resulted in his finding himself confined to his bed, and as he lay gazing at the ceiling he felt disappointed and a little ashamed that he wasn't as strong as other boys.

"Can't I go back to school?" he asked his mother one day. She patted the hand that lay on the coverlet. "The doctor thinks you should rest for a long time, Jamie. Not always in bed, but at home anyway."

"I was learning to read," he said half to himself. His mother, sensing what was in his mind, reassured him. "And read you shall—I'll see to that. You and I will read stories together. Your father can take care of the arithmetic, he knows all about that in his business, and he can teach you to write, too."

And so it was arranged, and soon Jamie realized that learning to read from his mother was more fun than it had been at school. Agnes Muirhead was an ardent Scotswoman, a descendant of the Lairds of Muirhead who had fought and bled for their kings. Her reading and storytelling were a little slanted in this romantic direction, but the words and sentences were the usual thing. The reading hours with his mother stirred Jamie's imagination, and before the year was out, he was able to read almost any book he could lay his hands on and, furthermore, make up and tell rather startling stories of his own.

His father's teaching of arithmetic was equally stimulating. James Watt, Sr., was a shipwright and ship chandler. He not only supplied the simpler things needed on board ships, but in his shop he produced the more important instruments used in navigation, which was becoming more and more important as the towns of Greenock and Glasgow grew as shipping centers. Arithmetic to Mr. Watt was a very practical, useful art, and that was the way he taught it to Jamie.

The hours in bed were, at first, merely something to be gone through with and forgotten. Then one day something happened that changed the whole picture. His little brother, John, aged four, was playing on the floor by the bed with a small toy cart. Accidentally stepping on it, he crushed one of the wheels, and like all four-year-olds he took it tearfully to the nearest person to be fixed, and this happened to be his seven-year-old brother. Jamie looked at the broken wheel, and the shattered pieces that fell off in his hand. The eager, teary face of his brother demanded some sort of action, and Jamie thought hard.

Then he had an idea. Beside his bed were some writing materials, including several pencils and a small knife with which to sharpen them. Very carefully splitting two of the pencils, he took out the graphite filling, making two shafts, flat on one side. Taking the odd wheel off the cart, he put it between the ends of the shaft with a pin as an axle, and fastened the other two ends of the shafts to the bottom of the cart. It was now rather an odd-looking three-wheeled affair, but it rolled along the floor, and closed the floodgates on John's tears. This success led to other experiments, and soon the hours in bed were filled with interest. Jamie was not only fixing his own and John's broken toys, but he was also creating new ones out of any that had been discarded. To use his hands this way was a new skill, and it fascinated him.

His father was much impressed, so impressed in fact that on his tenth birthday he gave Jamie a set of tools and set up a small forge in his shop for Jamie's own use. At first the workmen looked rather patronizingly at the young boy sitting by his forge. Then, instead of passing by and smilling, they began to stop and watch. For years Jamie had watched the men as they wrought capstans, pulleys, anchors and other heavy ship equipment, and now on the table beside his forge there began appearing models of all these things—formed with a precision that no man in the shop had ever seen before. "Jamie has a fortune in his finger ends" became the saying among the men.

Jamie enjoyed what he was doing. His isolation from other children had given him a very deep sense of insecurity. His newly found skill helped to lessen it a little, but he was still lonely. There was no doubt about that. He lived with his family and worked with the older men in the shop. His brother John, three years younger, was not particularly interested in what his older brother was doing.

Then along came Maggie. This was Margaret Millar,

Jamie's cousin, the daughter of his mother's sister. She was about Jamie's age and often came down from Loch Lomond to visit her aunt. Once Jamie had mended a doll for her. She had laughed at the idea of a boy using a needle and thread, and he had said, "Hands are hands. If they do honest things well, what difference if they belong to a boy or a girl?" Young as she was she had understood the wisdom of his remark. She had stopped laughing and smiled.

From that time on Jamie looked forward to her visits. Most children of his age embarrassed him. They were strong. They played rough games and, knowing his weakness, they never asked him to join them. Maggie, on the other hand, liked to talk, she admired the models he made, and even listened when he tried to figure some problem in geometry which his father was teaching him. She was often his companion on the walks he liked to take through the countryside. There was a hill near the Watt house covered with elms and beeches. It was a restful spot overlooking the house and the low-lying country beyond, and Jamie often went there to rest when his sick headaches made him tired and depressed. He even went there sometimes at night and watched the stars through the branches of the trees. It became a favorite spot for the two children when Maggie was visiting.

One June afternoon they were lying on the grass looking out over the countryside. The talk was of everything and anything. Thoughts pent up while Maggie was away surged forth when they were together. Even at ten Jamie was concerned about his own future. When he was well and could work in the shop or walk through the countryside gathering curious plants and flowers, or sitting in some humble cottage listening to tales of Scottish heroes, he worried less about it. When his sick headaches struck him they brought long periods of depression during which he could see no future but an idle half-sick existence.

"I know what I don't want to do," he said to Maggie. "I don't want to just sell goods in my father's shop."

"Maybe you could make some of the things he sells," she suggested.

"What they call philosophical instruments?" he asked.

"I mean the spyglasses and compasses and all those things they use on boats."

"Well, whatever it is, it's got to be something I can do well."

"I think you can do a lot of things well," Maggie said encouragingly. "Remember what you said about hands when I laughed at you for sewing up my doll?"

He nodded and the talk turned to what all Scotland was stirred up about—the escape of the Young Pretender, Bonnie Prince Charlie, as he was known affectionately to the Scots. In April, 1742, he had been ignominiously defeated by the English at Culloden Moor about a hundred miles from Greenock. It was his last attempt to regain the crown of Scotland, and with the final outcome of the battle no longer in doubt, the prince had disappeared. Prisoners, including many of his own officers, were taken and questioned under torture, but none admitted any knowledge of his whereabouts. He was reported seen in the most unlikely places; searching parties spread out all over Scotland to no avail. Rumors echoed from glen to glen in the Highlands, ricocheted off the slopes of Ben Nevis, swept across the still waters of Loch Lomond, and reached the ears of James Watt, Sr., and his family. Mr. Watt was a busy man and, being a prominent citizen, local matters took precedence over mere rumors national or otherwise. Jamie, on the other hand, was delighted. The romance of Prince Charlie, his bravery and his vaunting ambition to change the whole political face of England and Scotland intrigued him.

On this June afternoon he was listening to something that Maggie was saying about the rumors when suddenly her words became a mere blur of sound. Between the waving stems of the tall grass he saw something that brought reality to all they had been talking about. His house was clearly visible from where they lay and two men were walking up the path toward the front door, not an unusual thing in itself. These men, though, were unusual. They were not just ordinary men, not neighbors on a friendly visit, but men dressed in battered, mud-stained uniforms easily identified as those of the English army.

"Maggie," he whispered.

She crouched beside him and looked where he pointed.

"Lobsters!" she exclaimed in a shocked whisper, referring to them by the name universally used by Scotsmen.

"Aye," Jamie answered. "They'll no find him there. Let them search. The bonnie prince is too canny for such as them and—" A voice interrupted him. "Aye, Jamie, that he is." It came from behind and Jamie started to turn.

"Dinna turn round, laddie," the voice continued. "I want that ye should na lie when ye say ye've no seen me."

Uncomfortable as it was, Jamie froze in his position. The voice continued. "From your talk, I take you to be friendly. I want you to do something for me. Ye ken who I am?"

"Aye," Jamie replied. The Lobsters at his house and a man hiding left no room for doubt.

"I have not tasted food these two days. Can ye bring me a bit of supper when it gets dark? I've been following those Lobsters. They're moving south. By dark they'll be away. Would ye be afeered, laddie?"

What was happening fitted in with all the tales and legends he had been brought up on. Hidden in the thicket behind him was the most romantic of Scotsmen, Charles Edward Stuart. Furthermore he was asking Jamie Watt to help him. He glanced at Maggie who smiled. Then he answered unhesitatingly.

"No, sir."

"Ye'll be needing some excuse. I heard ye say just now that ye liked lying here looking at the stars wi' your spyglass. Bring it with you and lie awhile."

By the time the children reached the house, the soldiers were gone. Jamie very truthfully said he hadn't seen anyone, but before supper he confided in his mother. She was startled but as Jamie knew, the whole idea delighted her and she became a willing coconspirator.

After supper Jamie left with his telescope in plain view, but in his pockets and under his shirt he carried tasty bits prepared by his mother for Bonnie Prince Charlie. He kept his eyes and ears open but the country-side seemed quiet, and he reached the top of the hill without incident. As he passed the bush, a whisper told him to put the food under a low-lying branch.

"Then go off a wee bit and lie down wi' your spyglass," the voice added.

It was hard to concentrate on the stars, but Jamie did his best. After about ten minutes, the one-sided conversation began again.

"Ye'll no be hearing me again, laddie. Stay where ye are for half an hour. Then go home and say nothing." There was a movement behind the bush, then a pause.

"I heard ye talking wi' the wee lassie. A bit of advice I'll gie ye. Whatever you do as a man, be sure you really want to do it, and then make no mistakes. I wanted something and I failed because of mistakes that didn't have to be made." There was another short pause, and then a dark figure stepped out from the bush and disappeared down the path like a fading shadow.

TWO

Bonnie Prince Charlie walked down the path in the darkness and out of Jamie Watt's life. It was rumored that some months later a French boat picked him up off the Isle of Skye and carried him to France. Many of his followers were publicly hanged, protesting to the last their devotion to the young prince, and the matter became merely a fact of history.

To Jamie Watt it was much more. He felt himself to be a part of Scottish legend. All the stories that his mother had told him seemed to be summed up in this personal contact with a real Scottish hero. He treasured the words of advice, "Whatever you do as a man, be sure you want to do it, and then make no mistakes."

Jamie knew what he wanted to do—work with his hands, and furthermore he was trained not to make mistakes. His father had taught him the principles of geometry, and the exactness of that science of lines, angles and curves had always fascinated him. The result was that as the years went by, the models he made in his father's

18

shop became marvels of accuracy, so carefully did he avoid any mistakes in measurement or construction. The workmen began to count on him for perfection of detail in the more delicate of the instruments such as quadrants, sextants and compasses. When his father was commissioned by the Virginia Tobacco Company to produce for their ships the first crane ever seen at Greenock, Jamie was consulted. He insisted upon making a model before the final work was begun. No, there would be no mistakes in his work.

He was thoroughly contented and happy. He never went back to school and his days were spent in the workshop or walking through the countryside collecting specimens of rocks and flowers, or sitting in some peasant's house listening to the folklore that always intrigued him and that the country folk were only too glad to share with him. Maggie often joined him, and together they studied and classified the natural specimens that they picked up, poring over whatever books they could find.

Jamie's thirst for knowledge was insatiable. Before he was fifteen he had read two thick volumes of a book on natural philosophy, as science was then called, by a man named Gravesande, and at seventeen he taught himself German in order to be able to read a ten-volume work on mechanics by Leupold. "I have never read a book without learning something new," he said to Maggie, and together they read about astronomy, botany and even medicine.

So at eighteen Jamie was settled in a way of life that was pleasant and useful, so pleasant in fact that he had almost ceased to worry about his future. Then Fate made a few changes.

One evening after work the elder Watt called his two sons into his office. It was an evening Jamie never forgot. It had been a particularly burdensome day in the shop and his father was obviously tired. That there was something else on his mind was quite clear to Jamie. His father had always had a way of coming directly to the point, but this particular evening he sat for some time staring vaguely into a corner of the room. Finally he looked at both boys and began speaking rather falteringly.

"Your mother's not been well these past few months. Ye ken that?"

The boys nodded.

" 'Tis the will of God, lads, and I'm no complaining, but there's something else that's tied up wi' it that I don't think ye ken." He paused as though to emphasize what he was going to say. "I've just been informed of the loss of two of my ships. A lot of money was put into them. There'll be nothing coming out." The older man frowned and sighed. It was plain to see that what he had to say was painful to him. "Your mother needs care. I canna gie it to her and take care of two lads at the same time. Ye'll have to fend for yourselves from now on."

Faced with this ultimatum, decisions were quickly made. As Jamie knew he would, John chose an assignment as cabin boy on a ship out of Greenock. As for himself, there was not the slightest doubt. His inclination, his training and his skill all pointed to the trade of mathematical instrument maker, a very well-paid profession.

A cousin of his mother's, George Muirhead, was professor of Latin at Glasgow University, and he and his wife offered to keep Jamie with them while he looked for work. A job shouldn't be difficult to find, Jamie reasoned. After all, he had acquired a reputation in his father's shop, and he knew himself that he could construct many of the instruments in general use as well as the next man. This he found to his sorrow was only half the story. The mechanic workers of Glasgow were jealous of their skill and resented any outside competition. Jamie had not served seven years as an apprentice nor was he the son of a burgher. From their point of view he was a nobody, and no one would employ him. He walked from shop to shop and his spirits sank with each refusal.

Turning into a little side street one day, he heard the sound of a violin. Jamie had no ear for music, but the mere drawing of a bow across strings caught his attention. He looked up at the sign above the door through which the sounds came. It was made up of a huge pair of eyeglasses surmounting the word "OPTICIAN." Jamie went in. The shop was small and dim and at first he saw nobody. The sound of the violin stopped, and from behind a shabby curtain appeared a stooped old man carrying a violin.

"Yes? What can I do for you?" he asked. "Do you want a pair of eyeglasses?"

Jamie assured him that he didn't want glasses or a

violin or a flute or anything else that was for sale in the shop. All he wanted, he added, was a chance to work with his hands, and earn a little money. The old man shook his head discouragingly. Then as though a thought had struck him, he picked a pair of bent and twisted spectacles off the counter.

"Can ye fix these?" he asked. "My eyes are not so good and I canna see the wee pins."

Jamie looked at the spectacles. They were badly crushed, but his skilled hands soon had them straightened out. The "wee pins" that joined the eyepieces and handles presented no problem to his young eyes. The old man nodded over them in approval but made no job offer.

On the counter Jamie caught sight of a pile of vari-colored feathers, some thread and a tin of barbed hooks. He had an idea. All his life he had been fond of fishing, especially for trout and salmon. Perhaps he could impress the shop owner with a trout fly. Without asking, he set to work. Carefully picking out certain colors from among the feathers, he deftly tied them onto a hook. His companion watched him in silence and when the fly was finished he nodded again, only this time he added, "Ye make a braw fly. Ye can work here, but I canna pay much."

This was all the encouragement Jamie needed, and before many days had passed he was mending spectacles, making fishing rods and tackle and even repairing violins.

Jamie, of course, told the Muirheads about his job, but he was hesitant to talk of it too much. Most of the guests that frequented the Muirhead house were members of the faculty at the university. They were older men, and Jamie's natural shyness kept him from discussing what must seem to them a very minor lifework. There was one exception, Dr. Dick, professor of natural philosophy. Struck by Jamie's apparent interest in science, he drew him out with questions. Jamie's curiosity about everything and his desire to find out things for himself delighted the older man, and soon the two became very good friends.

Dr. Dick often visited the optician's shop and watched Jamie at work. One day, after seeing him repair a broken violin, he called him outside and out of earshot of the optician.

"Ye know, Jamie," he said, "ye're working here. That's fine. You've got a job. But ye're no learning anything. You can do better than repair fiddles. Take my advice, lad, and go to London. Talk it over wi' the Muirheads. If you go I'll gie ye a letter to a friend of mine."

Dr. Dick was very persuasive and Jamie took a day off to visit his father in Greenock and discuss the matter with him. Mr. Watt approved, but was a little skeptical about the money end of it. Jamie assured him that it was the experience he wanted. He would tighten his belt and live on next to nothing if necessary. Then, during the days of doubt, the matter was resolved in a tragic way. At the age of fifty-two, Agnes Muirhead died quietly in her sleep. It was a definite end to a period of Jamie's life, and he knew now that whatever any older people might advise, he must go up to London and learn to

stand on his own feet. "Whatever you do as a man—"
Bonnie Prince Charlie had said, and Jamie realized that
with his mother's death, he was about to find out what
that was.

Preparations were simple. A box of clothes, together
with his tools, was sent by ship from Greenock. Dr. Dick
gave him a letter of introduction to a friend of his, Mr.
Short, and a Mr. Marr who was going to London to join
his ship agreed to accompany him. On June 7, 1755, the
two set out on horseback from Glasgow. His father
pointed out to Jamie as they mounted their horses that
as far as he knew, no other Watt had ever crossed the
border into England.

Their route lay from Glasgow across to Newcastle and
down the east side of England by Durham, York, Don-
caster, Newark and Biggleswade. They used the same
horses for the whole distance, resting them over night
and all day on two Sundays. Jamie had a secret hope of
meeting with some highwaymen. Sixteen String Jack,
Jonathan Wild and others were still abroad to attack
unwary travelers. He was disappointed in this hope, although along the way they passed several gibbets with
dead highwaymen hanging limply, their powdered wigs
rain-soaked and bedraggled. So except for the loss of a
shoe and a resulting lame horse, the trip was uneventful
and in less than two weeks they arrived in London.

Mr. Marr left at once to join his ship, the *Hampton
Court,* a seventy-gun affair at anchor in the Thames
River. Jamie felt very much alone when he said good-
by to his friend. He put up at the Saracen's Head where

his box of clothes and tools would be delivered. After a good night's rest, he started out hopefully to sell his talents as a mathematical instrument maker. He went first to Dr. Dick's friend, Mr. Short, with the letter of introduction.

Mr. Short received him most graciously. After reading the letter, he sat for some moments before speaking.

"I have no wish to discourage you, Mr. Watt," he said finally, "but you'll not have an easy time finding work."

"But," Jamie protested, "Dr. Dick has vouched for my work and—"

"It's not your skill, Mr. Watt. I have no doubt of that if Dr. Dick vouches for it, but here in London the laws of labor are very strict. You're a stranger, you have never been apprenticed, and no instrument maker will take you."

Jamie's face fell. Where had he heard these words before? There was evidently little difference between London and Glasgow when it came to earning an honest living.

"But let me talk to a friend of mine," Mr. Short went on. "He is John Morgan, one of the best instrument makers in London, and furthermore a man of great character and understanding. Perhaps I can persuade him to take a chance with you."

The talk was successful. Mr. Morgan set Jamie a small task and watched his nimble fingers at work. He nodded to Mr. Short and agreed to take Jamie as an apprentice for one year, the boy to pay twenty guineas and give all his work free for that period. This was all very well, but the twenty guineas was a definite problem. Jamie was reluctant to ask his father for the money, knowing the financial difficulties that surrounded the older man. Finally Mr. Short persuaded him that with the instruc-tion he would receive and with his own skill, he would soon be able to pay his father back. Mr. Morgan, he pointed out, represented the only opportunity in all of London, and to turn the offer down would be fatal.

Jamie was convinced and wrote his father, assuring him that his ambition would be to become so expert that he would not only pay him back, but would be able to become an assistant in the shop and help take the business out of debt. The elder Watt's response was immediate, and Jamie was installed in London as an apprentice to John Morgan. He lived above the shop most frugally on eight shillings a week.

Mr. Morgan was a first-rate maker of mechanical in-struments for navigating ships and for surveying, and Jamie realized that here he could really learn to master his chosen profession. These instruments were all delicate and required the utmost accuracy in construction which was Jamie's specialty. In the long hours that he worked he learned the intricacies of quadrants, scales, dividers, azimuth compasses, sectors and theodolites.

One evening soon after his arrival, he went out to get a little air. Walking up Finch Lane from Mr. Morgan's shop, he was about to turn into Kettle Street when he heard a man cry out. The cry was suddenly muffled and replaced by a scuffle and a dull thud as though someone were being beaten. Jamie's first thought was to run and offer help, much as he disliked violence. Then he suddenly realized what was going on. It was undoubtedly the dreaded Press Gang. War was raging between France and England, and the British navy was desperate for sailors to serve its ships. They seized any young, strong-looking man they came upon, and Jamie knew only too well that should he be caught, his chosen career would be definitely closed.

No sooner had the thought struck him when the sound of beating stopped, and the clatter of running feet grew louder, coming in his direction. Finch Lane ended in a sharp turn up Cherry Lane from which the gang was coming. If they went straight across Kettle Street, they wouldn't see him, but should they turn up Finch Lane he would be caught. For Jamie this would be especially tragic; not only would it be an end to all his hopes and ambitions, but he would have absolutely no recourse to law. He was a stranger and somewhat illegally employed. No magistrate would even listen to any plea he might make.

It was too late to try running back to the shop, and there was no possible nook or post to use for a hiding place. He held his breath and waited. The gang reached the corner and paused as though uncertain where to go. Jamie's heart was pounding when an unexpected noise broke in. A window was thrown open and a bucket full of slops was emptied into the street. As the casement closed, the men moved off across Kettle Street, shouting curses at the householder who had spattered them.

From this time on Jamie stayed indoors at night. Since

he worked hard all day he was pretty confined, and his frugality in the matter of spending money "somewhat pinched his belly," as he wrote his father. His sick headaches became more frequent. He stuck it out for a year, but when his term was up he told John Morgan that he must return to Greenock. Morgan had to accept his decision since there was no other contract, but he regretted having to let so skilled a workman go.

Jamie laid out what money he had managed to save in some new tools which he knew he could not buy in Greenock, and in June, 1756, he reached home on horseback, just as he had started out a year ago, but with much new knowledge and renewed confidence in his own skill.

THREE

JAMIE WAS GLAD TO BE HOME FOR A NUMBER OF REASONS.
He preferred the Scottish air and the Scottish people to
anything south of the border, and he needed a rest. His
sick headaches and fits of coughing had grown almost
unbearable since he had been compelled to stay so much
indoors.

Furthermore—and Jamie made no bones about it—
he was happy to be near Maggie again. He had a lot to
tell her, not only of what he had done, but of what he
hoped to do. To talk to her helped to clear up any doubts
in his own mind.

No sooner had he gone to Glasgow, after a period of
rest at home, than he was faced with his first problem.
He had assumed that his training in London, and the
mechanical instruments he had shown himself capable
of making, would get him work at once. He was, however, curtly informed by the Guild of Hammersmen that
since he was not a native of Glasgow and had not

29

received his instruction there, no one would employ him.

This seemed incredible to him, and even Maggie could offer no solution. He spoke to his friend Dr. Dick about it, but there was no help there either. He knew, and this without any conceit, that he was probably as good a mechanical instrument maker as was to be found in Scotland and possibly in all of England. Mr. Morgan, in London, had been unable to teach him any more. He had, in fact, made a brass sector with a French joint that was not only better than could be made by another apprentice with ten years' training, but so superior that many who saw it commented on its perfection. He told Maggie that he wished he were a politician and could publicly fight the smugness of the Glasgow guilds.

Then from a most unexpected source there came a glimmer of light. One morning in 1758 Dr. Dick came to see him. Usually quite calm, the older man seemed oddly excited.

"Jamie," he said when the door had barely closed, "I've got you a job. It won't pay much, but it's a job." He sat down and took a deep breath before going on. "A verra rich man that ye dinna ken recently died in Jamaica. He had a superb collection of astronomical instruments and he left them all to the university. They arrived last night. They're badly rusted from the sea voyage, and some are broken. I talked to the committee first thing this morning. They want you to put the instruments in order. Will you do it, lad?"

To Jamie the question had only one answer.

"Of course I will," he replied without hesitation.

Dr. Dick wanted to be sure. "It'll only pay about five pounds," he said questioningly.

Jamie shrugged his shoulders and quoted an old Scottish proverb, "Many a mickle makes a muckle."

"You're a true son of Scotland, Jamie," Dr. Dick said laughing. "You will be hearing from me when we have a place for you. Since ye canna work in the city, it'll have to be in the university. We're free from town laws, ye ken."

And so it was arranged, and a few days after Dr. Dick's visit Jamie found himself ensconced in a small shop inside the university grounds. The astronomical instruments under his skillful care were soon put in order, and Jamie received the first pay in his chosen profession, £ 5 10ˢ 6ᵈ. This was not a fortune, but attached to the official payment was a formal notice appointing James Watt Mathematical Instrument Maker to the University of Glasgow. Jamie was established.

With his first job completed, Jamie began to wonder where any other substantial work would come from. The few small repair jobs he did for the science professors took very little time and brought in equally little money. But there was a bright side even to that. He enjoyed talking with the professors when they came with some small mechanical problem. He came to know such men as Adam Smith and Joseph Black. These men, in turn, began to realize that Jamie was far more than a mechanic.

His reading lessons with his mother had inspired in him a love of books, and over the years his store of knowledge on all subjects had become enormous. Adam Smith was professor of moral philosophy, an intricate subject, and had just become internationally known for his book, *The Theory of Moral Sentiments,* yet Jamie talked with him as easily in his field as he did with Dr. Joseph Black, professor of medicine, or any of the other staff members. They accepted him as one of them, and Jamie was soon on terms of real friendship with them.

He had become extremely proficient in making an instrument known as a "quadrant." It was used for plotting a ship's position at sea by measuring the angle of the sun with the horizon, and was originally invented by Sir Isaac Newton. During the first year, Jamie and a young boy helper turned out three a week, selling them for 28^s 6^d. When it was seen that the quadrants of Watt's were cheaper and better made than others, even members of the Guild of Hammersmen purchased them.

The sales became more than Jamie and his young helper could handle, and in 1759 he persuaded John Craig to enter into partnership with him. Together, they produced not only quadrants, but optical instruments, compasses, violins, flutes and even fishing tackle. The business was steady and Jamie had been able to pay his father back for the money advanced in London, but he was restless. When working on a quadrant or some other instrument he found himself wondering where it could be improved, but turning out the required standard ones each week left little time for experimenting.

Then one of those things happened that curiously

change a man's life. Among the many men connected with the university who frequented Jamie's workshop was John Robison, a graduate student in the field of natural philosophy. He was about the same age as Jamie, and the two men talked together most freely about their mutual interest in science. Robison saw in Jamie, as did the professors, a potential beyond that of a mere mechanic.

"Leave all this construction to others, Jamie," he would say, "and put your mind to creating something new." Then he would point out how the very quadrant that Jamie was building had been improved from such early instruments as the cross-staff and astrolabe, and that even as they were talking a new form, known as a sextant, was coming into use.

"Take the power of steam," he said one day. "I've been watching the model of the Newcomen engine in Professor Anderson's classroom. As you know, it is used only for pumping water out of mines. The thought occurs to me that this power might be used to move carts or other wheeled vehicles along our highways."

Jamie laughed. "What would we do with all our horses?" he asked. Then he became serious. "It's an interesting thought, John. Have ye any ideas how it might be done?"

"That's what I leave to you," Robison replied. "Obviously, the present up-and-down motion of the Newcomen pump must be made into a rotary motion. It's a neat little problem, but, as I say, I leave it to you."

Jamie worked on it. After his regular day in the shop, he would draw designs and put together crude models. The idea fascinated him, but his knowledge of steam was limited and the models he made would not accomplish what he and Robison wanted. He must find out more about steam. Here was power that might be adapted to an infinity of uses, but before considering its application, all its characteristics, weaknesses and strong points must be studied.

The idea haunted Jamie. He read about early experiments with steam. He learned how an ancient tribe of Teutons on the Weser River worshiped a stone god that periodically emitted clouds of steam accompanied by explosions. Long afterward it was discovered that the head was hollow and capable of holding nine gallons of water, and that the mouth and a hole in the forehead were plugged with wood. At appropriate times the priests placed live coals in the skull. As the steam from the heated water expanded, the wooden plugs were forced out with a loud noise, and the innocent worshipers prostrated themselves before their steaming god.

All through history, he learned, men had been conscious of the power of steam. They used it chiefly for amusement as in the aeolipile a hundred years or more before Christ. This was a hollow metal ball with protruding arms, which, when filled with water and heated, revolved as the steam came out of small holes under the arms.

It was all fascinating and Jamie would gladly have

devoted all his time to it. He disliked not seeing a problem through, but he had his business to think about, and even with John Craig and two apprentices to help, he was kept busy. He did steal time to make some experiments with what was known as a "digester." This was a device, invented by a Frenchman named Denis Papin in 1679, for raising the boiling point of water, but even this had soon to be abandoned.

Jamie had acquired a reputation for being able to do anything, and his friends took advantage of it. In 1672 a Masonic lodge in Glasgow was in need of an organ, and Jamie was asked to oblige. Had those who asked him taken the trouble to inquire, they would have found that he had absolutely no ear for music. They simply asked him, and he simply said yes, and this was enough: Jamie Watt could do anything.

He had worked on organs in London with Mr. Morgan, but he had never done more than repair the mechanical parts. The complete construction of one was a problem he had never faced, but he had given his word and the job must be done. The actual mechanical work, the pipes, the stops and the strings and wires to operate them presented no problem. He even improved on them by creating regulators for the strength of the blast of air, since he had always felt that organs were altogether too loud.

The question of tuning the organ gave him some sleepless nights until John Robison found a book in the university library that he thought might help. It was *Har-*

monics by a Robert Smith of Cambridge, and as far as anyone knew, it was the only book of its kind in print. There were chapters specifically on organs, but in his thorough way, Jamie read every page. He learned of the theory of the beat of imperfect consonances, which meant merely that to tune an octave of seven notes one had only to strike a note and count the beats or pulsations between it and its fourth or fifth. When these were reasonably even for each note, the octave was in tune. By this he was able, in spite of his ignorance of music, to tune the organ to any desired key.

The organ was a sensation. It brought him very much into the public eye, and more orders came to his shop than he could handle. It seemed that everyone wanted something repaired, from organs to guitars, and it was clear that his present setup was too small. He and Craig decided to move into the city, as he had been in business for seven years which satisfied the legal angle.

Besides, Jamie had a very personal reason for making a move to better quarters. He and Maggie had decided to be married. It was no sudden decision. Maggie had always been the one person Jamie turned to with his problems, his hopes and his ambitions. And so it was that on July 15, 1764, a notice appeared in the parochial register in Glasgow to the effect that "This day were married, James Watt, merchant, and Margaret Millar, lawful daughter to Daniell Millar, wright."

They moved at once into a house on King Street, Glasgow, where Jamie had his shop. It was a simple house, comfortable without any special luxuries, but Jamie was happy in it. He had his work, and he had Maggie always with him. Knowing Maggie as well as he did, he had no doubt that she was contented, too. The university continued to make use of his skill as a mechanic, and he might have gone on indefinitely with his instrument making. Then Fate stepped in again.

Jamie had never really lost his interest in steam from the time Robison had put out the idea of driving wheeled vehicles by steam power. One day in talking with Robison he learned that the small model of the Newcomen engine which was used in Professor John Anderson's science classes had broken down.

"It's a pretty model," Robison said, "and gives the students a good idea of the real thing, but it has never worked consistently, and some weeks ago it broke down completely. It was sent to John Sisson in London to be repaired. He is, as you must know, the best instrument maker in London, yet I hear he has given it up as hopeless."

"And why did ye not try me?" Jamie asked with a quizzical smile.

"Well, I suppose the committee figured that your business took all your time," was the answer.

"Repairing things *is* my business," Jamie protested. "Why, they even brought me an organ." There was a slight pause, and then Jamie asked, "What is the college going to do about it?"

"I haven't heard," Robison replied, "but if they get

it back from Sisson, would ye have time to look at it?"

"And why not?" was the instant reply. "Maybe I'll learn something about steam."

And so the little model of the only workable steam engine in the world was sent for to be officially turned over to James Watt for repairs.

FOUR

UNLIKE JOHN SISSON, WATT HAD A DEFINITE INTEREST IN steam. Robison had started and then Jamie had experimented with the Papin digester. In a vague way he recalled being fascinated as a child by the steam that came pouring out of his aunt's teakettle. He had, he remembered, caught some of it in a silver spoon and it had turned to drops of water. It was just a plaything then and he had all but forgotten it, but here it was again. A strange air with a quality of elasticity actually being used as a force to draw water out of mines, and with undreamed of possibilities for the future.

It took time for the little model to be carefully packed and shipped by coach from London, and James took full advantage of it. His business kept him busy by day, but in the evenings and often far into the night he read by candlelight everything he could find on the subject of steam or mechanics. He read through *A System of Hydrostatics and Hydraulics* by Stephen Switzer, a famous expert on gardening who was loud in his praise of Savery's engine for pumping water into the gardens of the rich. James refused to let language be a barrier and taught himself enough French to be able to read the books of two great engineers, John Desaguliers and Bernard de Belidor.

There were times when his headaches became unbearable and he had to close his eyes. Then Maggie would read to him, stumbling a little over some of the scientific words, but reassured by smiling explanations from Jamie.

Together they learned how a Frenchman, Salomon de Caus, used steam to create a little jet of water, a rather useless toy that the Marquis of Worcester later elevated to the dignity of a fountain. They read of Thomas Savery, who in 1698 combined the suction of the atmosphere with the force of steam and produced a fairly workable engine. Then there was another Frenchman, Denis Papin, with whose digester James had already experimented. Papin's engine was the first to use a piston with an up-and-down motion in a tight cylinder. The up motion was produced by expanding steam which was then condensed by chilling the outside of the cylinder, thereby creating a vacuum that permitted the piston to fall. Finally, two Englishmen, Thomas Newcomen and John Cawley, using the principle of Papin's engine, made a few changes and produced what had been known, since before Jamie was born, as the Newcomen engine.

Maggie read the words and Jamie visualized the characteristics of steam and the scientific principles underlying each new experiment. Steam, he realized, acted in two distinct ways. In the toy of De Caus, the motion it created came from its force and the natural reaction; in the piston type of engine such as Papin's and Newcomen's, the motion was created by the power that steam had for expanding in all directions.

By the time the little model reached Glasgow, Watt was quite prepared to diagnose its difficulties with intelligence. The day it arrived, he put it on his table and sat back and looked at it.

It was, as Robison had said, a "pretty model." Anyone unfamiliar with such things would have agreed to this, but in point of fact it was not a good model. It was intended to be built to scale. The whole affair, with water cistern, model beam and pump, was mounted on a simple black frame, and stood about two feet square. The diameter of the cylinder was 2 inches and the piston had a 6-inch stroke. The boiler was 9 inches in diameter which was out of all proportion to the amount of steam required to move the piston in the cylinder.

James soon realized this, finding that even when he blew on the small fire under the boiler, he was able to generate only enough steam for a few strokes. The answer must be in the boiler itself. Heat must be escaping. He checked the joints, but it was clear that the expert hands of John Sisson in London had already taken care of any defects here. It was clearly a matter of loss of heat by conduction and radiation.

In an attempt to prevent this, James made an outer wooden covering for the boiler. This seemed to help a little, but he felt sure this was not the only answer. By the time he had reached this point on the first night of experimenting, his candle had burned low and the pain in his head was bothering him. He went to bed pondering over the problem, and had a strange dream of being shot through a tiny hole by stinging hot steam.

The next night he lit fresh candles and prepared another experiment that had occurred to him during some of his waking moments the night before. Inside his boiler he inserted four or five brass flues so that he could be sure that he was using all of the heat coming from the hot furnace gases produced by the consumption of fuel. Then he went a step further and covered all the pipes that carried the steam with a nonconducting material or "lagging" as it was called. All this took time. Much of the work had to be done several times; slight corrections had to be made; hours were given to thought and calculation, and from time to time James had to give in to his headaches.

After a few weeks of this, he felt that he had ironed out the rough places in the boiler setup. The engine functioned better, and for class demonstration it was probably good enough. But "good enough" didn't satisfy him and he persuaded Professor Anderson to let him keep the model a little longer.

He turned his attention next to the engine itself. It was a new type. His interest in steam power had centered around the pumping engine of Thomas Savery. In this engine which had been in use some fifty years, water was either forced out of mines or into houses or gardens by the pressure of the steam alone. The Newcomen engine presented quite a new approach. The actual pumping out of water occurred when a vacuum was formed under the piston which then dropped, forced down by the weight of the atmosphere, and at the same time pulling up a container of water at the other end of the double arm or beam. The weight of the air was thus the final motive power—truly, James thought, an atmospheric engine. This was really the only new feature, the piston having been used by Denis Papin.

He went carefully over every part of the engine, making adjustments wherever he thought necessary. The tiny cylinder was checked for leaks. He made sure that the piston fitted as tightly as possible, that the injection and exhaust valves were in smooth working order and that the cradle arm was properly balanced. It was all done with meticulous care.

Mechanically, the little engine seemed sound, but it didn't altogether please him. He turned his attention to the steam itself. It was generated in the boiler, driven into the cylinder where it did its work of assisting in raising the piston. It was then condensed by a stream of cold water injected at the base of the cylinder. The resulting water was run out through the exhaust valve, leaving a vacuum for the piston to fall into. It was all simple enough and seemed to work without a hitch, but his keen eye noted some things that confused him.

In the first place, he was astounded at the enormous amount of water used in condensing the steam. It seemed to him to be all out of proportion to the amount of water represented by the steam in the tiny cylinder. Furthermore, when the water was ejected it was far hotter than was to be expected. Finally, he noticed that the injected water never seemed to condense the steam completely. There was always a little left, enough to weaken the force of the descending piston.

The first and second difficulties puzzled him. Why should steam at 100° C. require so much more water than its original volume in order to condense? Why, when it was condensed and ejected, should it still have so high a temperature? He lay awake night after night trying to figure out a logical answer. Could it be, he asked himself, that steam was at a temperature higher than the boiling point of water? His thermometer didn't show it, but what else was he to think?

A problem to James Watt meant an experiment, and he went to work at once. He bent a glass tube at right angles and inserted an end horizontally into the spout of a teakettle. The other end was immersed perpendicularly in well water contained in a cylindrical glass vessel. Steam was passed from the kettle through the glass tube until it ceased to be condensed and the water in the glass vessel had become nearly boiling hot. When this point was reached, James found that the water in the glass vessel had gained an addition of about one sixth part from the condensed steam. This seemed to prove, he thought, that water converted into steam can heat about six times its own weight of well water to 100° C., or till it can condense no more steam.

This was remarkable if it were really so, and he repeated the experiment with the utmost care. The results were approximately the same. He discussed the problem with John Robison who suggested that he talk it over with Dr. Black who had already done some research in the matter of heat.

"Jamie," Dr. Black said when he had listened to the problem, "it is strange that you should ask me that question. Some time ago I burned my arm in some steam from a kettle. That's not an unusual thing to have happen, but what set me to thinking was that the burn was far worse than any I had ever experienced with boiling water. I asked myself the same question you did. Could the steam actually have a higher temperature than the boiling water?"

"And ye found an answer?" Jamie asked eagerly.

"Aye, I did," Black continued. "Back in 1758, I noted one day that the temperature of steam from boiling water which, as you know, is 100° C., was also 100°. This didn't really surprise me until I began to reason. It took a long time and a large amount of heat to convert all the water into steam. It occurred to me that there must be a quantity of heat that escaped in the steam of which the thermometer gave no record."

"But that was only a supposition," Watt put in.

"True," Black replied, "and I don't like unproved suppositions any more than you do, so I tried an experiment. I took a hundred pounds of water at 60°, and I blew into it one pound of steam, making one hundred and one pounds. I took the temperature and found it to be 72°, a rise of 12°, then I took another one hundred pounds of water and added one pound of water at 100°. To my

astonishment—and here is the proof I know you are looking for—this water at 100° C. raised the temperature of
the one hundred pounds of water at 60° to only 62°."

"So the one pound of steam heated the water six times
more than the one pound of water at the same temperature?"

"Exactly," agreed Dr. Black, "and I think that was
your finding, or approximately so. Considered as the
cause of warmth, we do not perceive its presence. It is
concealed, and I have given it the name of 'latent heat.'"

With his own findings verified by Joseph Black, James
went back to his model. This loss of latent heat was, he
felt sure, the most serious defect of the Newcomen
engine. The volume of steam heretofore supplied for
each stroke of the engine was greatly in excess of the
content of the cylinder. A lesser volume, he reasoned,
would take advantage of this newly found latent heat,
and at the same time consume less fuel, a very definite
expense factor.

With the few changes he had made, the model was
working better and Professor Anderson was ready to
take it back to his class. However, James was not through.
Like an eager hound with a live scent in his nostrils, he
was going to track down all the weaknesses in the engine,
and since Anderson wanted to use the model as it was,
there was nothing for it but to build one of his own.

Dr. Black had been intrigued by James's questions
about heat and he was enthusiastic about the idea of
building a model. In fact, his interest went so far as to

offer to help in any reasonable expense that might be involved. With this encouragement and using the crudest materials—syringes from a pharmacy for cylinders, hollowed out canes for pipes, and thimbles from Maggie's workbasket as stoppers—James began construction. He was back at his favorite trade, expert mechanic. There was one difference; now he was combining his mechanical skill with the knowledge and reasoning of a scientist. It had been enough for Newcomen that his engine worked fairly well, but James was made of different stuff, and Maggie's enthusiasm gave him added spirit.

He built slowly, thinking out each step carefully. He used the general design of the Newcomen engine, correcting faults as he went along. He made the cylinder larger and more proportionate to the boiler. He found by experiment that one cubic inch of water produced eighteen hundred times its own volume of steam, a further proof of Black's theory. His boiler was encased in wood and had five brass flues extending through it for more perfect heating.

There was another phase of the whole project that also puzzled him. In order to create the vacuum under the piston, a stream of cold water had to be injected. This, as he had already noted, naturally cooled the walls of the cylinder. When, as the next step, steam was driven in, much of it was wasted in heating the now cool cylinder walls. Engine efficiency, James was sure, depended upon the steam entering from the boiler as hot as possible and remaining so throughout the whole process. But this appeared to be impossible since it was absolutely necessary to introduce cold water in order to condense the steam and create a vacuum.

As if this wasn't enough of a problem, there was the further difficulty that at best all the steam was never completely condensed, and the little that remained acted to prevent a complete stroke of the piston. To overcome this, Watt threw in a greater amount of cold water. To his surprise this seemed to retard the stroke of the piston more than ever. At first this stumped him. Then he remembered a discovery only recently made by Dr. William Cullen, professor of Chemistry at Edinburgh University, and some other philosophers. The gist of this was, he recalled, that if the pressure of the air above water is altered, the boiling point of the water alters with it. If the pressure is lessened, the water will boil at temperatures below 100° C. That must be, he told himself, exactly what was happening, since in a partial vacuum the air pressure would be far below normal.

It was one thing to become aware of the reason for something that happened, and quite another to overcome the resulting difficulty. A vacuum had to be created, but it seemed that the very creation of it hindered the efficient working of his engine. What, Watt asked himself, was the answer?

FIVE

JAMES'S INSTRUMENT BUSINESS WAS DOING WELL, AND WAS paying him a yearly salary of thirty-five pounds, besides profits from sales. He was able to leave it pretty much in his partner's hands. Even if he neglected it a little himself, he felt he must go on with his engine.

He thought of it now as his engine. Had he not conserved heat in the boiler by surrounding it with wood and introducing brass flues? Had he not discovered the waste due to that mysterious factor which Dr. Black had named latent heat? Furthermore, he had carefully determined in theory the quantity of water which a given weight of coal would convert into steam, and the weight of steam expended at each stroke. Indeed, he told himself, it was his engine in everything but name.

There was one great defect in it. Power was being lost through the cooling off in the process of condensing. It seemed like an insurmountable defect since cold was essential to condensation. He dreamed about this prob-

49

lem at night, and during his waking hours he thought of little else.

All his problems including this one had been merely of making improvements in a fire engine, of refusing to be defeated by some aspects of nature, a challenge not to be side-stepped—certainly not by James Watt. But assuming that he solved this latest problem and his engine should be flawless—what then? Would he have anything more than an efficient pump to remove excess water from mines?

Not, of course, that this was to be belittled. Far from it. From Edinburgh through Newcastle on the Tyne River, Sheffield, Manchester, Dudley, Cardiff in Wales and on the tip of the Cornish coast there was a string of coal, copper and tin mines, and others were being opened. The application of coal coke instead of wood charcoal for the smelting of iron was coming into vogue, and as much coal was needed as could be produced. The mines must go deeper and an engine to pump out the water was a vital asset.

But at this point, urged on by Maggie's enthusiasm, James's imagination took wing. Why should not steam power be used wherever wheels went around or mechanical force was needed? There were foundries now tied in closely with the production of coal, and the huge bellows and hammers had to be moved somehow. The tilt hammer that was used to forge hot iron was now worked by a horse on a treadmill, a fairly reliable but weak form of power. Why could not steam be substituted for the horse, and why could it not supply the blast for the furnace and work the rolling mills?

Woolen and linen goods, which for years had been produced in isolated cottages, were beginning to be made in centrally located mills. A man named John Kay had invented what he called the "flying shuttle" which enabled one man to make a much wider piece of cloth, and only this year, 1765, James Hargreaves had devised a way of spinning a dozen threads at a time. These were improvements, Watt said to himself, but they all required the power of a man, an animal or the vagaries of wind and weather. Could not his engine, with its defects remedied, be a source of power that could take the place of all man power, animal power, or water power? His ideas had no limit.

Robison had started his interest in steam by proposing its application to wheeled vehicles. He had made a crude model that had turned out to be impracticable—but on second thought, why not? There were the canals of Scotland and England which were being enlarged and extended as industry grew and there was real need for transportation. Watt visualized barges propelled by steam moving goods rapidly the length of a huge interlacing canal system.

All these would remain dreams until his engine was perfect, and right now it was far from perfection. There was a vital mistake somewhere that must be rectified. Prince Charlie's admonition to want something intensely and then make no mistake kept recurring to him. The young prince had wanted desperately to rule England and Scotland, a tremendous ambition that was frustrated at the last moment by faulty leadership—a most costly mistake.

Where was the mistake in the steam engine? Day after day Watt went over the working parts of his model, checked and rechecked each process and tested the theories behind them. The expansive power of steam, the latent heat it contained, the effect of the change of boiling point in a vacuum—all were tested time after time. He took long walks as he had done as a boy, hoping the solitude of the countryside would help to bring an answer.

Then, early in the year 1765, on a bright Sunday afternoon, the answer came. James had gone for one of his walks and Maggie was at home preparing dinner. She always took special pains over meals for him. His headaches still bothered him and his strength must be kept up. Suddenly the door burst open and James stood on the threshold, as Maggie told friends afterward, like a victorious Scottish chieftain, not slightly stooped as was his wont, but erect and proud.

"Whatever is it, Jamie?" she asked in surprise.

He took both her hands and sat her down in a chair.

"Maggie," he said breathlessly, "I've got it. It came to me just now. The answer we've been looking for. It's all clear, Maggie, darlin'." He had to pause for breath.

She patted his hand. "Now, Jamie, take a deep breath and tell me from the beginning."

"Well," he went on, "I was walking along thinking of

my engine. I had got to the foot of Charbottle Street and gone through the gate onto the green. You know the herdsman's house a little beyond the gate?"

"Yes, yes, Jamie," Maggie answered with kindly impatience, "but the answer?"

He smiled. "I'll never forget that spot, Maggie. That's why I'm telling ye about it. Ye'll just have to forgie me. It was right there that it came to me. Smack out of the blue. Now, listen carefully. Steam is an elastic body, isn't it?"

Maggie nodded, although not too sure of what he meant.

"Well, being elastic," he went on, "it will rush into a vacuum. Now, here's the answer. Oh, Maggie, I'm sure of it."

Maggie smiled patiently.

"If a communication is made between the cylinder and a separate—mind ye, I said separate—exhausted vessel, the steam would rush into it. Then it would be condensed without cooling the cylinder. In this way the cylinder will always be as hot as the steam that enters it."

Maggie was a little bewildered by the whole thing, and a little teary-eyed by James's enthusiasm, but she smiled and nodded.

James slept well that night although he did have a few dreams. The next day he was up early making drawings and calculations. He knew well that there would be other problems to solve before he had his perfect engine, but he was sure that the basic idea was sound. He had found the mistake.

First of all, it occurred to him that since his cylinder was to remain at the temperature of steam, he could not use the power of atmospheric pressure as Newcomen had done. The atmosphere, being cooler, would naturally lower the temperature of the sides of the cylinder. Therefore he decided to close the top of the cylinder except for a well-packed hole through which the piston would pass, and surround it with steam. He would then rely entirely on the natural force of steam plus the vacuum below or above and the weight of the machinery to give the working power.

Then, again, Newcomen had used water to keep the sides of the piston tight to the walls of the cylinder. This also had the effect of cooling the cylinder. James tried various fats and oils and finally made use of the steam itself. The whole engine must be kept hot. The size of the boiler, cylinder and condensing vessel had to be carefully figured, remembering the disproportion in the Newcomen model.

A final problem faced him in connection with the condenser as he had begun to call the new vessel. After the steam was condensed, the resulting water and any air must be ejected to make ready for the next stroke of the engine. He decided to do this by means of a common pump which could either be worked by hand or synchronized with the movement of the piston.

These essentials being determined and drawn on paper, Watt prepared to make a model. He secured from a pharmacist friend a large brass syringe for his cylinder, making a cover and bottom to it of tin plate. He was quite in his element in making the various parts such as the piston, the connecting pipes and the stopcocks. A small hand pump to evacuate the condenser was easily come by.

He put the brass syringe, or what was now the cylinder, on a small tripod in the middle of a wooden bench. The condenser consisted of two pipes of thin tin plate ten or twelve inches long and about one sixth of an inch in diameter standing perpendicular and communicating at the top with a short horizontal pipe of large diameter. This had an opening on its upper side shut by a valve opening upward. These pipes were joined at the bottom to another perpendicular pipe of about an inch in diameter which served for the air and water pump. The whole thing was placed in a cistern of cold water.

This stood next to the cylinder, with the hand pump in position to evacuate the water and air. To the bottom of the piston he attached a cord which passed through a hole in the bench, and carried at the end a weight of fifteen pounds. On the floor he set his small furnace and boiler. When the steam was generated in the boiler it was led by a pipe to fill the space above the piston. Another pipe led from the top of the piston to the condenser, and could be opened or shut by means of a stopcock.

When he was ready for the experiment he created with his hand pump a partial vacuum in the condenser. Then, when he judged that the space above the piston was full of steam and free of air, he opened the stopcock and permitted the steam to rush into the condenser, thus forming a hot vacuum space above the piston. This was now the high point of his experiment. No sooner had all the steam rushed into his condenser than the piston shot to the top of the cylinder, carrying with it the fifteen-pound weight on the end of the cord. This fifteen pounds represented the work done by one stroke of the engine.

But Watt was not completely satisfied. The whole thing was such a totally new idea that one experiment was not enough. He built a larger model on the same principle, but he made the condenser out of a single tin can instead of the two pipes. To his delight the engine now raised a weight of eighteen pounds on one quick stroke.

He couldn't wait to show the results of his experiment to his friend Dr. Black, who had helped him with the cost of the materials. Together they watched the action of the engine.

"Are you satisfied that this will work on a large scale, Jamie?" Dr. Black asked.

"Perhaps not just as it is," Watt answered. "You'll notice that I have inverted the cylinder so that the working power is the upstroke. I have a feeling that on a large engine I shall have to reverse this and use a working beam with the power or lift on the downstroke. But the principle will be the same. Except for that change, yes, I am practically satisfied."

"Why 'practically,'" Black asked.

"Because," Watt went on enthusiastically, "I have an idea that steam power can be applied both to the up-stroke and the downstroke, and I don't honestly believe we are getting the most out of the expansive characteristic of steam. But I'll try this first."

Dr. Black was impressed, but he was a very practical man. He pointed out that the cost of producing a large, working engine would be considerable. He didn't say this with any idea of discouraging Watt because he was deeply interested in this new steam power himself. But having already put considerable money into the small model, he well knew that the expense of a large engine would run into a considerable number of pounds, money that he himself could not possibly supply.

Watt thought the question over for many days. There were so many problems that he wanted answers for. The smoothing out of the cylinder, the better packing of the piston, and the more perfect condensation of the steam. These were uppermost in his mind, but he realized only too well the truth of what Dr. Black said.

His first baby, a boy named Timmy, had just been born, and what funds he had must go mainly into family expenses. To really solve the many problems of his engine meant constructing a large one. But how to do it without more funds? He could not ask his father who was already deeply in debt, and besides, not very well. Dr. Black had been generous in the past, but the thousands needed now were way beyond his means, and Watt was not one to impose on friendship.

He was frustrated. He was only twenty-nine and he had in his hands the secret of a successful fire engine— or steam engine as he preferred to call it. With it he could transform the whole pattern of life in England and

Scotland, and perhaps in the whole world. Yet for the want of a few thousand pounds he had to be contented to sit and look at a pretty mechanical toy that lifted eighteen pounds a few inches off the floor.

SIX

JUNE AND JULY OF THAT SUMMER WERE MONTHS WATT would never forget. Steam, steam, steam. The thought of it filled his mind and haunted his dreams. A power that worked without man's efforts—strong, reliable and cheap. He visioned wheels moving all through Scotland, England, Wales and the American colonies, all driven by the power he had found a way to harness. He realized that there must be improvements with vast new possibilities, that the end had not been reached, but he felt he had the secret in his separate condenser. Other things would follow.

His living was not expensive. It was frugal as both he and Maggie wanted it with true Scottish thrift. They lived above his workshop a short distance from his instrument business, and they were happy. Then three particular things happened to destroy their peace. John Craig, who had been his partner in the instrument business died rather suddenly. Watt had counted on him to carry the work along, as he knew too well that he himself was no businessman, and now the responsibility was suddenly thrust upon him. To make matters worse, the relatives of John Craig started a lawsuit over amounts due them on account of the partnership, and Watt, being unable to cope with it properly, found himself owing much of what little profit came from the business.

Little Timmy was a fragile child, even more so than James himself had been when young. The doctors were generous, but bills did come in to take away more of an already depleted income. Finally, Fate had brought the vision of steam power, a vision that Jamie and Maggie knew only too well could not materialize without a great deal of money. The vision had to be turned into engines and these would have to be manufactured in quantity.

Nights of sleeplessness or confused dreams, days of calculations, drawings, adjustments, repairs, ideas suddenly conceived, tried and discarded. There were desperate moments of inaction when his throbbing head forced him to close his eyes and try to forget his problems. Maggie was there always with kind words of encouragement, and Dr. Black a frequent visitor, but there seemed to be no answer.

Then toward the end of July, Dr. Black, on one of his visits, brought hopeful news.

"Ye've heard of the Carron Iron Works, laddie?"

Watt certainly had. It was Scotland's first iron foundry, opened only a few years before by a man named John Roebuck, some eighteen years James's senior.

"Well," Dr. Black went on, "I met Dr. Roebuck the other day through a friend of mine. It seems he has just leased the coal pits at Borrowstoness from the Duke of Hamilton, intending to use the pit coal, instead of the usual charcoal, in his foundry. We got to talking about coal mines and the eternal problem of water in them. The Borrowstoness pits are getting pretty deep, and at such depths the Newcomen engine is almost useless. I told him of your engine and—"

"Not about the new condenser!" Watt put in, fearful of his device of a separate condenser being made known too freely.

"No, no," Dr. Black reassured him, "not in any detail. I merely told him that your engine was much more powerful than the Newcomen. He seemed vastly interested, and asked me to have you get in touch with him. Why not write him? He is a man of the strictest honesty, and you can trust your secret to him." Dr. Black paused, then added with a smile, "I think he needs your engine, and I'm sure you need his backing."

Watt was ready for any attempt at a solution of his difficulties, and after talking it over with Maggie, he wrote Dr. Roebuck, explaining the new principles under which he proposed to construct an engine, and adding,

—I have tried my new engine with good success, for though I have not been able to get it perfectly airtight from its bad materials yet, immediately on turning the exhausting cock, the piston when not loaded, ascended as quick as the blow of a hammer. I have set about a larger and more perfect model, having now no doubt of its performing to satisfaction.

Almost immediately he received a reply from Dr. Roebuck.

Dear Mr. Watt,
   I am delighted to hear from you of your ingenious
device for the perfection of the fire engine of which
your friend Dr. Black gave me a few hints. It should
certainly prove of great value to all coal producers and,
as a natural consequence, to the whole iron industry.
Do please pursue your investigations whether as a
philosopher or a man of business. When you are ready
for a trial in the large, inform me at once. In the meanwhile let me hear of your progress.
                                        Your friend
                                        John Roebuck

With such interest shown, Watt decided to come to
the point at once. He wrote Roebuck offering him a two-
thirds interest in any patent he might secure for his
engine. In return he asked Roebuck to take over his
present indebtedness and assume responsibility for the
costs of other experiments toward perfecting the engine.
It was difficult for Watt to write the letter for, as he put
it to Maggie, he had always been totally unable to make
any bargain in money matters. Business was quite dis-
tasteful to him, and even after he had sent the letter to
Roebuck he felt that he had worded it badly and his
suggestion would be turned down.
   On the contrary, only a few days later Dr. Roebuck
wrote him agreeing to the terms and urging him to complete an engine model, even though imperfect, and then

secure a patent. With this encouragement Watt set to work with renewed vigor.

First he reviewed the situation. His engine had three basic points. There was the boiler to create the steam, the cylinder containing the piston in which the steam did its work, and the separate condenser in which the steam from the cylinder was destroyed. The boiler he felt was adequate at the moment. He had ideas about it, but they could wait. He looked at his cylinder. The first one he had used had been a brass syringe and this had pretty well served its purpose, but in his second model, which was larger, he had had to make it out of tin, beating it into shape with a hammer. The result was great irregularity in the inner sides. This permitted the steam from the boiler to creep around the edges of the piston where it was of no use and obviously wasted, making it necessary to use far more steam than needed and hence more fuel.

Newcomen had used water, too, but this water, being cooler, defeated his purpose of keeping the cylinder at the constant heat of steam. He tried wax, tallow and other convenient grease but steam still seemed to pass the piston. Somewhat in desperation he made collars of cloth thoroughly varnished. He tried two and then settled on four. He adjusted them one above the other around the piston, finding to his delight that the cloth seemed to adapt itself remarkably well to the uneven sides of the cylinder. Furthermore, with several collars, if some steam got past one it was taken up by another. There seemed to be a little friction caused, and after several experiments he settled on collars of oiled English pasteboard made of old ropes. This seemed to solve this problem.

Having made his piston almost perfectly steamtight, he turned his attention to the amount of steam consumed in each stroke of the engine. Obviously, he said to himself, the more steam consumed, the greater the cost in fuel, and the less practicable the engine.

To test this he applied a weight to the piston greater than it could raise. Then with a vacuum above it he admitted steam from his boiler. Having everything motionless he was able to observe more accurately. From the moment that he opened the steam cock to admit steam into the vacuum, until steam first appeared at the snifting valve, indicating that the vacuum was filled, was less than half a second. This seemed as satisfactory as could be desired.

The third factor in his engine—his own particular device, the condenser—being something quite new needed to be carefully studied. His very first one had been a tin can and one of Maggie's thimbles, but there had been much thought since then. He had tried making it of a series of thin tubes or small pipes, not more than an eighth of an inch in diameter, immersed in cold water. This he had changed to thin interstices between plates. Sixteen plates of a foot square he had figured would be the equivalent of nine hundred of his one-eighth-inch pipes, and far simpler to make. Unfortunately, these came unsoldered very easily and he fell back on the single vessel with an internal injection, much as the cylinder had been in the original Newcomen engine.

In October, 1765, he sent the finished model to Dr. Roebuck at Kinneil. In an accompanying note he admitted that while it was far from perfect, it was at least better than when he had started experimenting. With his working model in the hands of Dr. Roebuck Watt felt that the future was brighter. Roebuck had relieved him of most of his debts, and the engine represented a means of paying him back.

Watt had become rather a fatalist. The chance repairing of some astronomical instruments had led to his connection with the University of Glasgow that in turn had led to an established place in which to work. Then the failure of the Newcomen engine model had aroused his interest in steam, and now Dr. Roebuck had unexpectedly come into his life to make that interest a concrete reality. His troubles seemed to be over.

In the early part of 1766, Dr. Black came to the house on one of his frequent visits. He was obviously not his usual cheerful self. After greeting Maggie and asking after Timmy, he drew Watt aside.

"Jamie," he began hesitantly, as though feeling for the right words, "there is something you ought to know, and I don't feel that I am violating a confidence when I tell you. Dr. Roebuck is in serious trouble financially."

"But he agreed to—" Watt began.

"I know," Dr. Black continued with a slight shrug. "Dr. Roebuck is a generous man, and I'm sure he thoroughly believes in your ideas about the fire engine, but he has an outstanding fault. He is a speculator, and not a very wise one. He bought the Borrowstoness coal fields without realizing how much they were going to cost him in new equipment, and now he is up to his neck in debt. He has paid off your debts, but at great cost to himself."

"If my engine is a success—" Watt began.

Dr. Black interrupted him again. "'If' is a big word, Jamie. Let's face facts. You have the patent to pay for. Besides, you have only a model. A full-scale engine is an expensive thing, as I said some time ago."

Watt was stunned. As if it weren't enough that the lawsuit over John Craig had put him in debt, that the doctor's bills were piling up, and every day expenses were getting harder to meet. Now, the man he had counted on to help him was in trouble himself. The only thing he had to set off against all this was an idea, infinite in possibilities, but as yet developed only in model form.

It made no difference how deeply he or Dr. Roebuck believed in it or how great were the dreams of its potential. It was still only an idea until it was patented, built and sold. The first step was to get money, and Watt set to work. His instrument business was still a going concern, but without John Craig it was not turning out products enough to allow for any substantial profit. These would have to come from some other source.

SEVEN

From the days when Watt worked for his father and then through his own mechanical instrument experience, he had become thoroughly familiar with instruments used in surveying.

His passion for exactness of detail and precision of workmanship was common knowledge to his friends. He had all the qualities for the work of surveying and map making, lacking only actual experience. It would, he told himself, be a natural profession to turn to. There was one great difficulty of which he was aware. He had an inborn dread of meeting people, of making bargains or giving orders. As a small boy during the few months he attended school, he had been a solitary figure incapable, even if not unwilling, of joining the other boys in games or arguments. He knew only too well that to go into business as a surveyor and civil engineer meant dealing with all sorts of people—hiring, firing, arguing, persuading—and the thought terrified him.

Besides this, there was his engine. Above all, he must

work at it and perfect it. In good faith Roebuck had paid him money for the patent and this must be secured at once, or others would steal his idea. It was a difficult situation but, putting aside his personal prejudices, Watt decided to accept what seemed the only solution.

In the summer of 1766 he opened an office on King Street, Glasgow, not far from his home, advertising himself as a land surveyor and civil engineer. Except for the great John Smeaton who had just rebuilt the Eddystone Lighthouse on the rocky coast of Cornwall, there were very few of this profession who amounted to much, and Watt was quite optimistic.

The first week went by and he sat in his office waiting. It wasn't time really wasted, though, because he covered sheets of paper with drawings of new ideas for his engine. He was beginning to feel that not enough use had yet been made of the expansive power of steam. He toyed with the idea of using two exhausting barrels instead of one, giving each of them half the stroke, thereby producing a more perfect vacuum, and he drew a rough plan to introduce steam on the downstroke as well as the upstroke.

Then suddenly tragedy struck, and all thought of his business or steam or anything else was given up. His second child, little Jenny, was barely three months old when Timmy caught cold and, in spite of frantic efforts, died in his mother's arms. It was hard for the father to realize what had happened. He had always wanted a son, and now to have him taken away was almost more than he could bear. He stayed at home to comfort Mag-

gie and help with the baby, but by the third week he was
back in his office. His spirits were at a very low ebb,
when one of the local magistrates came to see him.

Would Mr. Watt be willing to take on a small job of
surveying for a short canal from a nearby coal field to
the city of Glasgow? Concealing his enthusiasm, Mr.
Watt indicated that he would consider it. Of course, the
magistrate took pains to point out, the city was not in a
position to pay a very large fee. Watt shrugged his
shoulders as if to indicate that the honor of working for
the city of Glasgow was worth any fee, and the deal was
closed. Watt knew perfectly well that in a sense he was
a bargain to the city, that John Smeaton would have
demanded a far higher fee, but who was he to quibble?
He would do a good job, make a little money and perhaps gain a reputation.

The job, as the magistrate had pointed out, was small,
but Watt put his best into it as was his nature. He enjoyed the field work while surveying the route, and the
work in the open air tired him just enough to make him
sleep soundly at night. When it came to the question of
contracts, rights of way and the usual bargaining, Watt
muddled through unhappily. By the end of the year, the
job was done and he pocketed the small but welcome
fee of a hundred pounds, and turned again to thoughts
of his engine.

John Roebuck had said nothing in detail about his
financial troubles and still urged Watt to carry on until
he could build and patent a full-sized engine. He had a
full-sized cylinder cast at Carron, convinced that until

a cylinder was cast and not hammered, there would always be a waste of steam. Unfortunately, the first one cast at Carron was useless, as the boring turned out not exactly vertical, and it was therefore impossible for the piston to move freely. All this took time, and 1767 was well along when one day in August the magistrate again approached the land surveyor's office with a new proposition.

They wanted a survey made for a canal to connect the rivers Forth and Clyde from Stirling through Loch Lomond to Dumbarton. Watt knew this country well and agreed to do the work. What he didn't know at first, but found out later, was that he had a rival working on a similar project. John Smeaton had been engaged by another group of subscribers to survey the same general area, and this was pretty stiff competition, but every shilling was important and he wouldn't let himself be frightened off even by the great John Smeaton. He made the survey and submitted it with cost figures. Then it developed that since he had a competitor, it would be necessary for him to go to London and appear before a committee of Parliament on behalf of the subscribers to his plan. It was the sort of assignment he hated. It meant arguing and persuading, but there was nothing else to do.

"I want you to stop in Birmingham, Jamie, and see a friend of mine," Dr. Black said to him a few days before he left. "He is Dr. William Small, a most ingenious fellow. I think you two should get along well."

This was said quite casually, but like many casual remarks it led to something very vital in James Watt's life.

The journey to London was made by coach and Watt couldn't help thinking back on his first trip there in 1755 on horseback. "The first of the Watts to cross the border," his father had said. The business in London was soon finished as the committee of Parliament found that the route proposed by Smeaton was shorter—and less expensive with fewer locks, and he was therefore granted the contract.

Watt was somewhat disappointed, but he consoled himself with the thought that he had at least earned a small fee and that he now had time to get back to making experiments on his engine. "Never," he wrote to Maggie about the Parliamentary committee, "have I seen so many wrongheaded people on both sides."

He had promised Dr. Black that he would look up Dr. William Small in Birmingham, and a two-day coach trip took him the hundred miles from London to the sprawling manufacturing town on the river Rea. Dr. Black had sent a message to Dr. Small and Watt was expected. He found his new friend a man slightly older than himself, a successful physician with interests far beyond the limits of his profession. He had been, up until 1765, professor of mathematics and natural philosophy in the college of Williamsburg in Virginia where he had a rising young colonial, Thomas Jefferson, as a student. Since that year he had been associated with Matthew Boulton who had established the largest manufacturing plant in England, where he produced works in steel, plated goods, silver and ormolu, or imitation gold.

Knowing Watt's interest in the mechanical arts, it was only natural that Small should suggest a visit to the factory at Soho just outside of Birmingham.

The factory was two miles out of Birmingham. It covered an enormous area, far greater than the foundry at Carron. The main building, rising from the valley which concealed the lower of its five stories, was relieved of its plainness by a wide, overhanging roof pierced with dormer windows. Circular towers lent it a castlelike appearance, its true nature being shown by the smoke billowing from its two tall, fingerlike chimneys.

Watt was impressed, and as Dr. Small led him from room to room and he saw the skilled workmen fashioning heavy bowls of silver and steel, and delicate ornaments and jewelry of brass, he was seized with an idea. These men were artists. He watched them work, noting the precision of touch of which no workman he had ever used had been capable. The mistakes in his model engines had always been due to faulty workmanship at Carron. Somehow, he told himself, his engine must be made in this factory.

He mentioned the idea to Dr. Small who was interested but noncommittal, indicating he might speak to Boulton about it. He urged Watt to secure a patent before doing anything.

All the way back to Glasgow, the vision of the Boulton factory stayed in Watt's mind. If he could only get Mr. Boulton interested enough to go into some sort of partnership with Roebuck and himself, he felt that the success of his engine would be assured.

Of course, Roebuck would have to agree, but Watt felt sure that with his affairs in such a bad state, he would accept any offer. He spoke to him about it and, to his surprise, Roebuck hesitated.

"You have something, Jamie, that will make us both rich men. There is no reason why we can't together, without anyone else, bring this thing to a successful end. Get a patent, Jamie, then we'll build a full-sized engine, even if it isn't perfect."

With both Small and Roebuck urging the need of securing a patent, Watt decided to go down to London again to take the matter up with the authorities.

The pain of little Timmy's death had been somewhat relieved by the birth early in 1767 of another son, named after his father and nicknamed 'Jemmy,' and in 1768 a daughter named after Maggie. Then, as though Fate would not allow Watt a full measure of happiness, just as he was about to leave for London, his first daughter Jenny developed a severe congestion of the lungs that proved fatal. The inherited weakness was taking its toll. He and his wife were going through the same period of sorrow that his parents had suffered. The simple funeral was a point of dedication for them.

Jemmy and Margaret must grow up. No pains must be spared. The success of his engine and his surveying work became more important than ever. The agony in his mind must give way to material action, and the first step was, obviously, to assure protection for his invention.

Securing a patent was not an easy thing to do. There

was a feeling in government circles that a patent was monopolistic. What right, many argued, did any man have to be the sole beneficiary of anything that was for the good of all. The routine was that application had to be made and what were called "letters patent" issued. This protected the patent applicant for four months, during which time he had to produce detailed specifications. At this point the courts put every possible obstacle in the way, throwing out applications because of some vague word or phrase. It all seemed unfair to Watt, but he had to comply with the law.

During the next few months, he visited offices, talked with important men in white wigs and black gowns, and unimportant men with no wigs and shoddy knee breeches. He wrote letters, appeared before committees, argued, protested, gave in here and there, but never gave up. In spite of headaches and sleepless nights he persisted, and finally on January 5, 1769, letters patent were issued for "A New Method of Lessening the Consumption of Steam and Fuel in Fire Engines." This was merely the general principle and protected Watt for four months. He was now faced with the problem of writing out detailed specifications.

Two days of rest refreshed him somewhat, and he took the coach for Birmingham. He had two reasons for the trip. He wanted to actually meet Matthew Boulton, and he needed Dr. Small's help in making out the specifications for his patent.

Mr. Boulton had been told of his visit by Dr. Small,

and received Watt graciously at his house on Hounds-
worth Heath near Soho. There were other guests including Dr. Erasmus Darwin, a man slightly older than
Watt, a poet, doctor and botantist, and a Mr. Keir, a
skilled writer in the field of science. It was just the sort
of company in which he felt at home, and the fortnight
Watt spent at Boulton's house raised his spirits and gave
him new confidence. Dr. Darwin in particular appealed
to him. His tastes and accomplishments were as catholic
as Watt's. The four men listened eagerly to his account
of his new "fire engine," and his dreams of what it might
accomplish for England. When it came to a question of
the specifications which had to be prepared for the government, both Small and Boulton warned him of the
pitfalls.

"You can't go into too great detail," Dr. Small insisted.
"That will just make it easier for anyone wishing to
pirate your ideas, and don't think for a moment that there
won't be many such people."

Watt was a stickler for detail and this advice puzzled
him.

"But how will anyone know what I'm patenting if I
don't give details," he protested.

"Let me make my point clear," Dr. Small explained.
"Take your steam vessels, cylinder pipes and piston;
these must always remain at an equable heat. Now don't
specify any special method of doing this. Use such terms
as "proper materials" to cover them with or the application of heated bodies when they may be wanted. The

same wording should be used in the case of your separate condenser, your air pump and the use of steam instead of air on the downstroke."

With this sound advice Watt carefully prepared his specifications, handed them to the proper authorities and returned to Glasgow, steeling himself for a long wait. This did not mean idleness, and he set to work at once on new ideas for his engine.

He concentrated on the condenser, feeling that it was the heart of the whole project. The condensation of the steam must not only be rapid in order to increase the speed of the strokes, but it must be complete or there would be a loss of power as there was in the old Newcomen engine. The pump must work with an absolute minimum of friction so that less force would be needed to run it and more force be left for the primary purpose of the engine.

He was encouraged by the success of these experiments and arranged with Roebuck to start construction of a full-sized engine at Kinneil. His dream seemed to be coming true as he began assembling the various parts.

He was all too conscious of the fact that everything he did toward the success of his engine was running him more and more into debt and making it harder on Maggie to take care of Jemmy and Margaret. Roebuck was, he thought, altogether too optimistic and he held fast to the thought that in some way Boulton and his factory should take over.

Then early in 1769 he received a letter from Dr. Small.

—and I have convinced myself of the generosity and integrity of Mr. Roebuck whose troubles are overwhelming. As for the engine, I have no kind of doubt of your success . . . whether it would be possible to manage the wheel and reciprocating engine by separate partnership, I am not certain; if it is Boulton and I would engage with you in either. I am in haste, dear Watt, your affectionate humble servant

W. Small

Light at a dark moment. Watt went at once to Mr. Roebuck. He knew before he went that it would not be an easy interview. Arguing was not his strongest characteristic, and Roebuck had already expressed himself very strongly against sharing any possible success with others.

"I've been reading the copy of the specifications you left me," Roebuck said as they sat down in his office. "Your friends Boulton and Small seem to have advised you well."

This seemed to be a perfect cue. "It's about them that I'd like to talk to you, John," Watt began. "I've just had a letter from Small and he seems eager to join forces."

"Of course he is!" Roebuck exclaimed. "He knows this engine will be a success and he naturally would be glad to share, but as I told you—"

A certain desperation gave Watt courage. "I know that," he said, interrupting, "but I'm thinking of it from our point of view, not his." He had started now, and he must finish. "Success for us can only come with money, and that we just don't have. Materials must be bought and men must be paid, and, besides, we have the patent fee to think of."

Roebuck was silent and Watt pressed his advantage.

"You and I can retain part of the rights," he argued. "Surely it's better to be satisfied with some success than to see the whole thing collapse."

With his own affairs in such a bad state, Roebuck knew in his heart that Watt was right. He paced the floor; he stood and looked out the window. Then he turned.

"All right, Jamie," he said in a tone of resignation. "I'll write to Boulton today."

EIGHT

Watt had grown very tired. The many months of experimenting with pipe condensers, plate condensers, drum condensers, steam jackets, piston bands, condenser pumps, exhausting cylinders and dozens of other engine problems had wearied him. He was as eager as ever to realize his dream, but he was haunted all along by the fact that he must have help from some outside source to relieve him of the burden of debt that had been daily growing heavier and heavier.

It was not only that he had a Scotsman's dislike of owing anyone money, but he saw his beloved family threatened with real suffering. Maggie had been through enough. The deaths of their children had been a bitter blow. Now Jemmy was two years old and little Margaret just a baby, and Watt intended to stretch every point to see that they had the best of care—but it cost money.

Now at last he had not only Small's letter assuring him of Boulton's interest, but Roebuck's promise to write and propose negotiations. He slept soundly that night. The

79

burden of worry suddenly became weightless. The control of steam was in his hands with possibilities almost beyond conceiving, and there were good friends around him to help him perfect it.

In spite of some recent improvements in the roads from Scotland to England, Watt knew that a mail coach to Birmingham would take at least two days to go each way. Then one had to allow for the possibility of highwaymen or some breakdown. Mr. Boulton and Dr. Small would need time to consider Mr. Roebuck's offer, and there was, of course, the chance that they might be away.

Time was never wasted in Watt's life, and he entered with renewed spirit on plans for the engine. Among other things, he had realized for years that in order to make his engine, which was reciprocating, practicable for millwork, its up-and-down motion must in some way be made rotatory. In his specifications for the reciprocating type, he had drawn out a scheme for securing this rotatory motion by means of a hollow wheel.

This consisted of an annulus or ringlike structure with three flaps hinged on the inner surface, so that they turned through a right angle and formed an abutment for the steam introduced and exhausted at the side by regulators. The passages communicated with the boiler and condenser respectively through the hollow axis. The other abutment for the steam was formed of mercury or Newton's metal, whose weight kept it at the lowest point while the wheel revolved under the steam pressure. This was ingenious, but Watt felt that it was too complicated, and therefore too expensive for practical use.

He remembered that once in 1768 when visiting a colliery at Hartley he had watched a method which made use of the piston and beam of the Newcomen engine. It consisted of a toothed sector on the end of the working beam, working into a trundle or small wheel which, by means of two pinions with ratchet wheels, produced a rotative motion in the same direction by both the ascending and descending strokes of the arch. This had worked, but clumsily and with great irregularity. Watt set his mind to work on some simpler method.

It had early occurred to him that the treadle and crank of a common foot lathe represented a logical means of transforming an up-and-down motion into a rotatory one. With this in mind he drew up plans and specifications for a model. Since he knew that before too long Boulton would be replying to Roebuck and he must be ready to try out this engine on a larger scale, he hired a mechanic to build the model. He worked with him for a while and then turned it over to him to finish. This workman, Robert Cartwright, was a trusted man from the Carron factory. He was to become one of Watt's many stumbling blocks, although neither knew it at the time.

One day at the end of February, 1769, the post arrived with a letter from Birmingham. Watt tore it open. He felt sure that here, at last, was the support that he needed. He read the letter carefully. Then he read it again because it was hard for him to believe what it said.

Boulton had indeed heard from Roebuck, but the offer was quite unacceptable.

"Dr. Roebuck," Mr. Boulton wrote, "has offered me a share of the property as far as respects the counties of Warwick, Stafford and Derby. This plan is so different from what I had expected that I cannot think it a proper one for me to meddle with. It would not be worth my while to make for three counties only, but I would find it worth my while to make for all the world."

So Roebuck was still the stubborn optimist. Watt was ready to sacrifice any of his share if he could only get the engine into practical use. On the other hand, Roebuck floated on a cloud of optimism, sure that he was in a position to bargain. This optimism was flattering to Watt in a way, but it struck him as very strange when he considered Roebuck's own financial difficulties which were fast piling up. Watt's every argument was constantly met with a smile and often the quoting of an old Scottish proverb, "Never bid the Devil good morning till you meet him."

The letter from Boulton, the latest in his series of difficulties left only one course open. Watt must make a definite trial of the engine even without the assurance of help. It was just possible that the added expenses with which he would be faced would bring Dr. Roebuck to the realization that he must make an offer acceptable to Mr. Boulton if he were to survive at all. The last sentence in Boulton's letter gave him a ray of hope. "I would be willing to make for all the world." This was also Watt's ambition.

Had he had nothing else to do, no other responsibilities, the erection of a trial engine would have been a labor of love, so confident was Watt of the value of his various inventions about to be consolidated in one huge engine. Unfortunately, there was the eternal specter of money. Since his work on the first Glasgow Canal and his survey for the Lomond Passage, he had acquired a reputation and his services were more and more in demand. Here was a sure way of earning much-needed money. He realized that he must put his engine second for a time, however much it irked him.

There was, on the other hand, nothing to prevent his having the work on the large engine started, and he discussed plans with Roebuck. It was at first planned to have it built in a large warehouse in the nearby town of Borrowstounness but Watt objected. There would be too many prying eyes and consequently much loose talk, things he wanted to avoid until the engine had at least somewhat proved itself. Piracy of his ideas was still a dread even though the patent existed.

Back of Roebuck's house at Kinneil was a sweep of wooded, rather hilly country, and by a little stream not far from the house was an outbuilding long unused and covered with vines. Here, Watt decided, was the ideal spot for his first trial. Roebuck rather reluctantly agreed, and assigned a number of his workmen to take orders from Watt. These orders were very definite. Watt knew what he wanted, and his experience with mechanics had shown him how inferior most of their work was. He longed for the skill and care he had seen at the Boulton factory, but he knew that he must get along with what he had.

Since he must be away on his surveying projects most of the time, he insisted that only certain things should be done. Many of the more delicate operations and the assembling of the whole, he wanted done only when he was there to supervise.

The boiler bottom must be laid first. There could be little bungling there. The supports for the great beam could be put up. He specified that these should be at least fourteen inches square and fourteen inches apart at the top to admit the iron strap that would secure the axis. The chains at each end of the beam could be made in his absence by the chain makers, but even here Jamie insisted that they should be made of the best tough iron that dusted easily, the middle link three quarters of an inch thick, the two side ones a half inch each and the breadth about three inches. The wood for the frame, he ordered, should be got ready but not put up.

With everything underway at Kinneil, he turned his mind to the all-important job of making a little money. The Glasgow magistrates needed his help. They had seen what he could do and they appealed to him again when they were faced with a problem. This was the cost of coal in the city of Glasgow. There was coal everywhere, but it had gotten into the hands of men who monopolized it and charged exorbitant prices for bringing it to the city. Watt was asked to make a survey for a canal to connect Glasgow with the coal pits at Monkland in Lanarkshire. If this could be done it would cut the cost of coal to the people of Glasgow by fifty per cent.

The logical route seemed to be a long valley between the pits and the city of Glasgow, but Watt found that there was a rise of over two hundred feet from the river. He then set about finding the shortest, fairly level route among the nearby hills. The usual method of measuring the distances was with a chain made up of one hundred links and about sixty feet in length. This was all very well on dry, level ground, but took much time and trouble when such obstructions as woods, rivers, lakes or marshes had to be crossed. There must be a better way and Watt put his mind to it.

In the eyepiece of his telescope he placed three fine hairs, one vertical and two horizontal and at right angles to the single hair. He then took a six-foot rod with two round disks, one fixed to the rod and the one above movable. Each was white with a horizontal red line, easily distinguished at a distance. He then sent a boy to a measured distance, the length of several chains, with the rod, and had him stand with it in a vertical position. He turned his telescope until the horizontal hairs in the eyepiece exactly covered the two red stripes at the same time as the vertical hair covered the line of the rod. As soon as this was accomplished he marked the rod into distances equal to the distance between the two red lines. He reasoned that if the boy should take the rod to an unknown distance, say across a river or a lake, the upper disk would have to be moved up in order that the hairs might cover the two red lines. The new distance could then be computed from the known measurements on the rod. When the boy stood at a distance too far to hear his voice he would indicate up and down by arm signals. After experimenting on short measurable distances, he found that his new method worked with a variation so slight as to be negligible.

At first the workmen smiled at him and his telescope, since they had no way of knowing that it would become the basis of all future surveying. They were used to dragging their chains through all sorts of obstacles, and an innovation like this, they thought, was just a young man's whim. Watt challenged them to compare measurements, and after several days they had to admit that time and effort were saved without any loss of accuracy.

This preliminary survey included the testing of soil at various depths, estimating the cost of cutting away hillsides and dredging lakes and streams, and, most difficult, negotiating with all sorts of people for the purchase of their land.

By October he had determined that a canal without locks was possible through the surrounding hills ending within one mile of Glasgow. It would, he estimated, cost ten thousand pounds. He submitted his findings to the proper authorities, pocketed his fee and turned again to his steam engine.

During the almost six months of his absence, his engine had been growing. In the quick one-day trips he made from the field he invariably found the workmen standing around doing nothing, generally because some misreading of his instructions had caused a minor failure which no one seemed able to remedy. But in spite of stupidity and indifferent workmanship, the engine had taken shape.

Following his instructions the copper base for the boiler was laid and the great boiler, five and a half feet at the bottom, erected over it. This was a giant compared to the models he had been working with. The eighteen-inch cylinder with an area of two hundred and fifty-three square inches was made of iron with a five-foot stroke, and was enclosed in another of wood to conserve the heat, the area between the two being filled with steam. The piston rod and wooden piston were set in place and packed with oil. The upper surface of the piston was in connection with the undersurface and with the boiler by a pipe through which the passage of steam was controlled by a hand regulator. This was a sector with two ports in it which placed the underside of the piston alternately in communication with the upper side and with the condenser.

Then came the heart of the whole engine, Watt's brain child—the separate condenser. He was by no means sure that this was in its final state. He had tried and planned a great variety of ways of condensing the steam. For this first trial, he was using the simplest possible. It was nothing more than a pipe with another concentric to it outside. It was made of hardened lead and was fastened to a wooden frame with a pump of tin eighteen inches in diameter and twenty-five feet high to evacuate the air and water. Finally the whole was crowned by the great beam that would raise the pump. He had given up the idea of a direct-acting pump.

He brought Maggie down the night before the trial, and they sat and looked at the strange monster. By candlelight it seemed like some apparition from a distant world, standing, cold and silent, in an abandoned outhouse. But it was his dream—the first steam engine ever built with a separate condenser. Would it work? Would it be more powerful and use less steam and fuel than the Newcomen engine which he always referred to as the common engine? Would it accomplish all the wonderful things that he hoped for? Would it transform the industrial world?

The year was 1769 and in London another man just about Watt's age, George William Frederick, better known as George III, was worrying about his American colonies, about his rather obstreperous Parliament, and about his dream for ruling the world by himself. As yet he knew nothing about the mild little Scotsman who was trying to transform the industry of England and the world. Watt was not particularly concerned with George's problems either, which left the two dreamers quite independent to dream toward quite different awakenings.

NINE

On September 5, 1769, Watt was up early checking every part of the monster. Dr. Roebuck and the men who had worked on the engine were to be the only spectators at the trial except for Mrs. Roebuck and Maggie.

What should happen was very simple. As the steam was generated in the boiler, it would pass into the cylinder until the piston was in equilibrium when the weight of the descending arm of the beam would carry it to the top, the steam below it would then pass into the condenser as the hand cock was opened. The piston would fall into the vacuum thus formed, carrying the opposite end of the great beam up with its load. Then the process would be repeated. The theory was quite sound. How about the practice?

The fire was started in the boiler. The small audience waited. They felt the heat on their faces as the boiler warmed up. As it reached the boiling point there was a hissing sound. From the plates surrounding the manhole door, and from around the screws that fastened the steam box to the wooden cylinder, jets of steam appeared. One of the men sprang up to stop the engine, but Watt held him back. Obviously there was a leakage, but it was not great and he knew it could be rectified later. There was undoubtedly plenty of steam in spite of this slight loss.

He was right, for in a moment the great beam tilted, carrying the piston to the top of the cylinder. The man at the regulator opened the valve that let the steam and air out of the cylinder into the condenser to permit the piston to fall into the vacuum thus formed. True to theory it started down, but after descending two feet it stopped. Steam was again admitted and the piston again ascended to the top. For a second time the air and steam were let out. Watt watched the great arm to which the piston was attached. In spite of the vacuum below it the piston descended only a few inches. It was evident that the vacuum was for some reason incomplete.

The engine was halted, and since there appeared to be trouble in the evacuation of the cylinder, Watt examined the condenser. He found that the leather on the outside of the oil pump bucket had, in some unaccountable way on the first stroke of the piston, been turned inside out. He put on a second piece of leather pinning it to the first. Then he turned to the cylinder. Here he found that the pasteboard collar of the piston had been torn. He replaced it by a three-ply oiled pasteboard instead of one.

Steam was again admitted. This time there was no immediate pause in the movement. The piston made five or six fine, brisk strokes. Watt caught a glimpse of the faces of the watching men. One or two smiled and nodded. The motion became slower. Finally it stopped altogether. The changes he had made had definitely improved the working of the engine. There must be something else. His heart felt heavy. Was this the end of his dream? It couldn't be, he reasoned. The theory was quite sound. There was no question of that. Besides, his own faith in the engine was backed by both Boulton and Small, even though they had refused Roebuck's offer. The trouble was definitely mechanical. This was something that could be solved by his ingenuity and perseverance, and these he proceeded to put to the test.

The whole engine was dismantled. Every part must be carefully examined to be sure it was doing its share of the work in the best possible way. It was found that oil was coming through the condenser. Investigation showed that the passage through which the oil pump should discharge the oil was far too small. The oil was thick, ropy and heavy and naturally slowed up the movement. When it remained in the condenser it lay on top of the water from the condensed steam. This water in the reduced pressure of the vacuum boiled violently and drove the oil out of the condenser. There shouldn't be this much oil anyway and Watt went carefully over the cylinder. He found that at one point it was oval instead of round, and of course the oil used to make the piston tight flowed past it. Future cylinders, whether cast or hammered of tin, must be quite round.

These were the kinds of problems with which he liked to be faced and he set his men to work on them at once.

He convinced himself, and Roebuck agreed, that the trial had not actually failed. The moments when his engine had worked smoothly at a brisk six strokes a minute were worth all the moments in which it had failed. As long as there was a remediable reason for the stoppage, there was great hope.

But there was the question of money. The workmen had to be paid, the materials were expensive. Roebuck was enthusiastic, but his affairs were becoming more and more involved. Credit could not go on forever. To persuade him to come to some satisfactory agreement with Boulton was becoming more than ever necessary. The faults in the trial engine were largely due to poor smithwork, but it was the best that the Carron foundry could produce. To get the truly best one had to pay highly. Matthew Boulton not only had the money, but he had the trained men. Watt himself had seen that. Roebuck's pride and optimism overshadowed everything.

The bright side of the picture was that there was a growing interest among the various town magistracies throughout Scotland in improving the system of canals and consequently the harbors of important towns such as Ayr, Greenock and Glasgow. His reputation as a careful surveyor had spread since his survey and estimate for the Monkland Canal, and a source of money was clearly opened to him. It meant, of course, that he would have very little time at home and that whatever improvements were to be made on his engine must be handled by the incompetent workmen at the Carron foundry.

His survey and estimate for the Monkland Canal had been presented to Parliament and a writ for its construction obtained. The authorities wanted Watt to superintend the whole project. He didn't want to do it. He knew it meant at least two years during which time any real progress on his engine was impossible, a discouraging outlook. But it was inevitable and he finally agreed.

Before starting, he had a long talk with John Roebuck. Certain alterations must be made in the engine. The descending valve of the oil pump must be considerably enlarged, the wooden piston must be replaced by one of cast iron and it must exactly fit the cylinder, which consequently must be perfectly round throughout its length. He explained his latest idea for his condenser which was to be equipped with two pumps.

"You know, of course, Jamie," Dr. Roebuck said, "that while I agree that all this must be done if our engine is to be marketable, I cannot at the moment be of any financial assistance."

It was the first time his partner had expressed anything but optimism, and Watt sensed the strain it was for him.

"I can pay for these improvements out of my fees from surveying, John," Watt assured him, "but what really concerns me is the future. Even supposing that we cannot make the engine much better than we have; it would work easily with eight pounds on the inch, and would not consume much above half the steam used by a common engine. It would thus be in demand, and we could sell. But we have to build before we sell, and where is that money coming from?"

"I made Boulton an offer and—" Roebuck began.

Watt interrupted him. "Matthew Boulton thinks in large terms, John," he said kindly, "and while your offer was quite genuine and businesslike, it was limited. The world is Boulton's only limit."

"And you think I should agree to any terms he might make? Is that it?"

The matter was out in the open at last and Watt was not going to mince matters.

"Boulton is too big a man, John, to propose anything unfair, and I feel positively that we must get this engine into general use even if you and I have to stand a loss. It's too important to be made a personal thing."

"I'm going to London this week," Roebuck said after a pause. "I shall make a point of seeing Boulton and Small and—well—we'll see."

This was enough for Watt. He put his instructions about the changes in the engine in writing and prepared to start his work on the Monkland Canal.

Fortunately, his field of work was not too far from home. He was able to see Maggie and the children from time to time, and also to drop in at Kinneil and check on the progress of the engine. It was hard for him to turn his mind to anything else, but the days in the field offered him challenges that compensated a little. The most level route had to be estimated, the soil at various depths tested, land had to be purchased from frequently unwilling landowners, and enemies made as a consequence. Rocky ground had to be dug up by hand, hillsides slashed and bridges built. He had plenty of men to do the physical work, but it was done grudgingly. From early morning till late at night, he rode his horse from one section of the work to another, listening to complaints, solving problems, most of which existed only because of the slovenliness of the work. Rain soaked him and cold froze him until with an aching head he was ready to give up.

Watt was unhappy with the human side of all this. The workmen were lazy. He found himself having to strike shrewd bargains without the advice of others, and in many cases he had to keep the financial accounts himself through lack of help.

"I find myself out of my sphere," he said in a letter to Dr. Small, "when I have anything to do with mankind. It is enough for an engineer to force Nature, and to face the vexation of *her* getting the better of him."

After two months in the field, he went home for a visit. He thought nothing of the life on horseback after his two long rides to and from London. He found Maggie, the baby and his year-old son well. Perhaps, he prayed, they would be spared the inherited weakness that had deprived him of Timmy and Jenny. He was doing everything he could to supply the necessary money, and Maggie was giving them the loving care that came so naturally to her.

There was a letter from Dr. Small. He remembered only too well how eagerly he had opened the last letter from Boulton, and how deeply disappointed he had been. He prepared himself for bad news and quietly opened the letter.

The first words reassured him: "Matthew and I have come to an agreement with Roebuck—" Dr. Small then went on to explain that Roebuck had agreed to turn over half his share in the patent to the Soho partners in return for a sum of money to be determined fairly among all. There were no strings attached this time, no limitations on the sale of the engine. It was destined for all the world, and it could now be built in the factory at Soho.

Watt felt as exhilarated as he had some four years before when the idea of a separate condenser suddenly became a clear image in his mind. He wrote back immediately, "I received yours, and shake hands with you and Mr. Boulton on our new connection which I hope will prove agreeable to us all."

This was all very well, but without him nothing could be done to perfect the engine. He was committed not only to finish the Monkland Canal, but had contracted for several other projects, a canal across the isthmus of Crinan and improvements to the harbors of Ayr, Greenock and Glasgow. He was strictly a man of his word. He was not his own master until these things were completed. Furthermore, in his letter Dr. Small had emphasized the fact that at the moment much of their funds were tied up in other projects. Obviously he must wait for Mr. Boulton before going into action.

For six months he labored. The canal grew slowly along its twenty-mile path. His fingers itched for action on his engine, but after all, he thought to himself, he was being paid, and with his salary of two hundred pounds a year, though not exactly kingly, he was paying off old debts and keeping his family in reasonable comfort.

In April, 1770, he received word that the engine with the improvements he had specified was ready for a second trial at Kinneil. He hurried there full of hope. Mr. Boulton had come up from Birmingham to see at first hand what he was to become financially interested in. Actually, he was thoroughly convinced of the rightness of the principle, but he felt that his presence would add strength to his words.

The trial was fairly satisfactory. The cylinder was more even and much less oil got through to interfere with the action. The piston was made of iron instead of wood, and alterations had been made in the condenser. The strokes were quite regular and continued for a longer time than they had in September. Whether Mr. Boulton was greatly impressed or not Watt couldn't be sure. His remarks afterward were pleasant but quite noncommittal as regarded the actual trial.

"I understand, Jamie," he said, "that you have plans to turn this vertical motion into a rotatory one?"

"I have ideas on that," Watt replied, "but I've been too busy in the field to really get down to it."

The reason I mention it," Boulton continued, and there was a note of uncertainty in his voice, "is that I'm afraid someone has gotten ahead of you."

Watt started. "I don't understand," he protested. "I have heard nothing of it."

"It's not likely that you would, Jamie," Boulton explained. "It has only just been patented. Small was in

London about some new idea for a watch, and a friend of his in the patent office, knowing his interest in such things, told him of it."

Watt's mind went back a year to the time when he was busy getting ready for the first trial of his engine. He had started a model of a rotatory engine and left it in charge of a mechanic named Cartwright. Could it be possible?

"Mr. Boulton," he asked, "would ye ken the details of that device?"

"Not actual specifications, no, but in general it—"

"Was it," Watt interrupted, "based on the theory of treadle and crank such as is used in a common foot lathe? Did it use two cranks at right angles to each other, working with two beams and two cylinders, the beams being equipped with weights which would act during the time of the ascents of the respective pistons?"

"Why, yes," replied Boulton, "that is just about what Small told me. How did you know?"

Watt couldn't suppress a slight smile. The situation appealed to his sense of humor. He felt it was rather crazily dramatic.

"Because I invented it," he answered. Then he told Boulton about the model which he had left in Cartwright's hands.

Both men were silent for a moment.

"You know, Mr. Boulton," Watt said finally, "the more I think about it, the more I reach the conclusion that the true inventor of the crank rotative motion was the man who first contrived the common foot lathe. Applying it to the engine was like taking a knife to cut cheese which had been made to cut bread."

"What do you intend to do about it?" Boulton asked.

"I shall hope to get an admission from Cartwright and then forget it," he replied. "After all, if anyone wants to use this patented device, they must first have our engine. I'll find a better way of doing it."

TEN

STEALING HIS IDEA WAS HARD FOR WATT TO UNDERSTAND.
He was instinctively honest and he had always felt that
other people were, too. While the shrewdness of the
various contractors and property owners on his surveying projects was irritating, it could not in all fairness be
called dishonesty. Cartwright's act—and Watt was convinced it was he who had stolen the idea—was as bla-
tantly dishonest as any thieving.

With Roebuck's help, he drew an admission from
Cartwright. He had, he confessed, told some of the
workmen at a neighboring mill run by a man named
Wasborough, what he had observed in his work on the
model. The man who took out the patent was the
Wasborough engineer, John Steed. Mr. Steed, when
faced by Watt, claimed that his invention was quite
independent. It was a point almost impossible to prove
and Watt refused to argue it. As he had said to Boulton,
if anyone wanted to use this rotatory principle they must
of necessity make use of his separate condenser which

100

was already patented. He dropped the whole matter. Cartwright was promptly discharged and a few years later hanged for highway robbery.

It had been an unpleasant experience, but it taught Watt a lesson. It was obvious that he must be more careful. His mind was teeming with new ideas for his engine. He must, he now realized, keep these to himself until he was able to patent them and protect them from pirates. Also, he must find time somehow to prove some of his theories by making working models. To do this he closed out his instrument shop, which was not exactly prospering anyway, and set the room up as a laboratory. He then arranged his supervision of the various engineering projects for four days a week, planning to devote three days to his experiments on his engine. The laboratory was on the same street as his home so it was all to be quite satisfactory.

But he underestimated his reputation as a surveyor, and for the next two years he had very little time to give to his engine or any experimental work in the laboratory. The seaport towns of England were growing in importance. Colonial trade was increasing. The harbors of such places as Ayr, Greenock and Glasgow must be deepened and made more navigable. There were other engineers such as John Smeaton and John Rennie, but Watt's careful work had won him an almost equal reputation, and in the region of Glasgow, he was, after all, a local boy.

Along with the improvement of the seaport harbors, the rivers leading into them had to be widened and deepened. The work was there and the money was there, and he plunged in. It was a choice, he told Dr. Small, between experimenting on the engine, the event of which was uncertain, or embracing an honorable and perhaps profitable profession. After all, he had no definite contract or even an understanding with Boulton. The agreement with Roebuck was entirely a matter of the ownership of a patent.

The Monkland Canal was well along but needed another year for completion. He gave it as much of his time as he thought necessary and spent the remainder riding horseback from one side of Scotland to the other. At Perth he surveyed for a short canal from that city northeast to Couper of Angus, and thence up the valley of Strathmore to Forfar. While this was being approved by the authorities, he journeyed to supervise the deepening of the river Forth, and to carefully check the building of a two-hundred-and-twenty-foot bridge of five arches across the Clyde River at Hamilton. While the authorities had him at Glasgow, they persuaded him to make a survey and report on the bed of the river which they wanted improved for the increased navigation which was expected.

Watt almost ceased to be a person. There was no apparent limit to what he was supposed to do. No sooner was the condition of the river bottom at Glasgow surveyed and reported than he was on his horse and off for a seventy-five-mile ride to the western sea where the authorities wanted a canal built across the isthmus of Crinan, then down the coast to Ayr, which was growing as a seaport and needed better harbor facilities. Who was better than James Watt to give them to them?

It was all flattering. It brought in money, but it was tiring. Exposure to the cold winds from the snowy Grampian Hills to the north of Perth gave him a bad cold and fever. The interminable riding over the rough terrain between Glasgow and Crinan and on down to Ayr brought a recurrence of his headaches, and the short rests at inns along the way were only inadequate respites.

He cheered himself by writing home and stopping for brief visits as he passed through the Glasgow area. It cheered him to find that Jemmy, aged six, and Margaret, a year younger, were in sound health. The curse of the family weakness had apparently passed them by. His friend Dr. Small in Birmingham was an enthusiastic correspondent, always eager for news about his various projects. Small was quite an inventor himself, having patented several types of watches, and the two men found much in common. He wrote Watt at one time that he and Boulton were trying to figure out some way in which the steam engine could be used to propel the barges which were being used more and more as the canal system of England and Scotland grew.

This idea intrigued Watt and he wrote back: "—and have you ever considered a 'spiral oar' for that purpose, or are you for two wheels." The spiral oar was a single screw of perhaps four spiral turns which, attached to the stern, would drive a barge through the water. He did not, of course, know that he was looking directly into the future. He promised himself he would look into it later when he had perfected a method of rotary motion that would not conflict with Steed's patent.

From the first moment that he had realized how much steam the Newcomen engine wasted, he bent his chief efforts to lessening this waste. The separate condenser had, of course, been spectacular in this respect, but once this was established as an integral part of his engine, Watt began thinking of other ways to save this precious element—steam. The less steam one used, the less fuel was needed, and fuel was expensive.

The idea uppermost in his mind was based on the fact that steam was an element that expanded. Why wouldn't it be possible, he thought, instead of using a great quantity of steam, enough, say, to fill the cylinder, to use only a portion of it in the cylinder and allow it to expand of its own accord to exert the necessary pressure on the piston? There were certain unanswered questions which would have to wait for actual experimenting. Just what percentage of steam could be omitted from the cylinder to produce an equivalent force, and how could this be regulated in case additional power were needed? These must be looked into.

Then there was what he called the double-acting principle. This was to devise a method of using the force of steam to drive the piston down as well as to push it up, instead of relying on the weight of the beam. The chains that connected the piston with the arm of the great beam never pleased him. They were awkward and did not always pull with a truly vertical motion. Finally, there was the best method of turning his reciprocating motion into a rotatory one.

His laboratory was waiting. He had only to finish his surveying commitments which had already greatly eased his financial troubles, and he could get to work. A letter from Small made him more than ever anxious to do this.

At present, I am to tell you of something of consequence. A friend of Boulton and me in Cornwall tells us that four or five copper mines are going to be abandoned because of the high price of coal. He begs me to write to him instantly about our engine. Also, the Yale Building Company delays rebuilding their engine, waiting for yours. Only yesterday application was made to me by a mining company in Derbyshire to know when you are going to be in England about fire engines, because they must quit their mine if you cannot relieve them.

As if this were not encouragement enough, he received a letter from his old friend of Glasgow University days, John Robison. Robison had been sent to Russia to direct the Imperial Academy of Marine and he wrote urging Watt to come to Russia as they had great need of his steam engine. "They are using," he said in his letter, "very expensive windmills to drain water from the dock basin. I feel sure that a well-paid position is awaiting you here, and I should, of course, like to have you near me."

Not only England, but the world! Here was a real demand for something that was not yet in production, something that represented unparalleled power, but lay, as impotent as a paralyzed giant, in an outbuilding at Kinneil. To make it vital it needed expert and conscientious workmen—and the money to pay them. In his mind the engine was more than just an idea. He had nursed it for more than six years and he knew it would work.

Through his friend Small, he prodded Matthew Boulton, but the answer was always the same. The huge Soho factory was too involved for the moment with other commitments to warrant taking on anything as big as the construction of steam engines. This did not imply any lack of faith on Mr. Boulton's part. It was simply that he was a very careful businessman and refused to take unnecessary risks. This was the secret of his success. He owned part of the patent. The engine would have to sleep and he would have to wait.

Apparently, Watt thought to himself, England doesn't altogether agree with Mr. Matthew Boulton. Valuable copper and other minerals would remain underground for lack of power to drain out the water that seeped in at low levels. It was a vicious circle. Coal was high priced because without an engine to pump out the water, fresh supplies could not be obtained, and the pumps could not be worked because the price of coal was so high.

Word had spread that this new engine, which few had even seen, could be run much more cheaply than the Newcomen. Pleas had come in from southernmost Cornwall as far north as Derbyshire for the new steam engine. Yet the man who had given a soul to a useless fire engine was incapable of answering these pleas, and had to spend his time building canals to transport the very things which were dependent upon his engine. It was frustrating.

In the early part of 1773, Dr. Small wrote Watt that a plan was being discussed by the Council of Trade and the Admiralty to make a passage for ships from Inverness to the western sea at Fort William by Lochs Oich and Ness. He urged him to make a survey, assuring him that great advantage would come to him in government circles. The only advantage Watt wanted was a chance to make the steam engine in quantity and to serve his nation and the world. The proposed survey was, he felt, just another delay. But in the uncertain state of things with Mr. Boulton, he and Maggie both felt that any activity was better than frustrating idleness, and he undertook the survey in August at the official request of the Court of Police.

It was an interesting project. It would affect the shipping not only from the east coast to the west coast, but also from America. Ships from the overseas colonies could steer around Ireland and cut through by the Irish Sea to Inverness with a great saving in time, and generally more favorable winds. Watt's enthusiasm grew during the first few weeks in the field. The country was wild, the terrain rough, and the constant rain kept him soaked so that it was hard for him to keep even his notebook dry, but it was constructive activity, and this he loved.

Then Sunday, September 26th, came around, a date he would never forget. He was resting at an inn in

Inverness after a busy and hectic Saturday in the field. Early in the morning the post brought him a letter from his father-in-law. Maggie was seriously ill, so seriously in fact that he was urged to come to Glasgow "with all speed." The letter was dated September 24th. He had already lost two days. There was no post chaise or coach until the next day, but he couldn't wait. Traveling by horseback had become a routine to him and besides, the weather being rainy and the roads full of deep ruts, a chaise could easily break down. A horse was surer.

That night he reached Fort William. He allowed himself and his horse the shortest of rests and early in the morning set out for Dumbarton by way of Tyndrum. On September 28th at ten o'clock at night he arrived in Dumbarton. He was still twenty miles from Glasgow and so tired that he was afraid to attempt pushing on. The weather had cleared somewhat and he ordered a chaise for the next day. His heart was very heavy. It was now four days since Maggie's father had written, and Watt had a dread foreboding. His beloved Maggie needed him and he wasn't with her.

About the middle of the next morning when he was about to set out, a chaise arrived from the south. It carried two passengers. One he recognized as Gilbert Hamilton, the agent for the Carron Company, and an old friend of his. As he got out, his worst fears were realized. Hamilton was dressed in somber black, but even if he hadn't been, the sadness in his face was sufficient. Yes, Maggie had died shortly after her father had written his letter. Hamilton had set out on the chance of meeting him, hoping perhaps to soften the blow.

Together they drove back to Glasgow. There was not much either of them could say. Hamilton suggested that they go directly to his house. Watt offered no objection. The thought of going home where there would not be the cheery welcome he always received from Maggie had haunted him ever since Dumbarton where he had learned the news.

Mrs. Hamilton welcomed him. Her sister Anne was staying at his house with the two children and the next day plans would be made for their future. The first thing was rest. Thoroughly exhausted by weeks in the field, the trip from Inverness, and the sad and confused thoughts in his head, he tossed throughout the night, but it could hardly be called rest.

The funeral was simple, attended by the many friends of the Watts. Afterward he summoned up courage to enter his house. He remembered so well bursting in eight years before and greeting Maggie with news of his condensing idea for his engine, and how her eyes sparkled with sympathetic enthusiasm.

It seemed to him that he could not possibly go on without her. What did success mean if not shared with her? They had always done everything together since they were children. For days he sat moodily by himself, or watching while Jemmy and Margaret played around him. They were his only link with Maggie and the past, and their future must be carefully considered.

It was arranged that Anne Macgregor would look after Jemmy and Margaret until he had fulfilled his contract for the Inverness Canal. After that, the family's future depended entirely on definite action on his engine from Matthew Boulton.

ELEVEN

THE END OF THE YEAR 1773 WAS A VERY DARK PERIOD FOR James Watt; so dark in fact that he was almost ready to give up. The Hamiltons and Anne Macgregor were kind. His gratitude for all this was immeasurable, but he was haunted by a fear of the future. He was obligated by contract to finish the survey of the Inverness-Fort William Canal which had been so cruelly interrupted, but what then? What of his engine? What of his dreams of moving the world's machinery by steam?

He was thirty-seven, and nine of those years had been spent in a ceaseless effort to improve his invention to, as he felt sure, the brink of success. Yet everything seemed to militate against it. Lack of money, indifferent workmanship, Roebuck's difficulties, his own health, the stealing of his plans, and now, harder than anything else to understand, Boulton's apparent indifference. He had taken a part ownership in the patent; he had paid off many of Watt's debts, and had shown a real interest in the steam engine, but it all ended there. In fact, he was quoted as having said that the engine was as yet "a shadow as regards its practical utility and value."

But Boulton was not as indifferent as Watt thought. He was merely a very shrewd businessman, and a perfectionist. If he went into a deal, it must be done in the biggest and best way possible. He was not a compromiser. In 1772 the firm of Fordyce Brothers, headed by Alexander Fordyce, failed after years of speculating. The current dispute with Spain caused severe fluctuation in the London stock market, and Alexander absconded with a hundred thousand pounds. With this crisis facing the commercial world, Matthew Boulton quite naturally hesitated to invest in anything new.

Then a tragedy brought things to a head. John Roebuck failed completely and was declared bankrupt. It so happened that Matthew Boulton was one of his creditors to the extent of twelve hundred pounds, and Watt suggested to Dr. Small that this should be a good time for Boulton to take over completely Roebuck's share of the engine in return for a cancellation of the debt. The mercantile crisis had become easier and the other creditors had no desire to take any part of the patent in lieu of payment, so Boulton agreed.

Watt felt deep pity for his old partner John Roebuck, but there was nothing he could do to relieve him. He knew in his heart that the truth of the matter was that Roebuck's failure, by spurring Boulton to take over, was a blessing though rather tragically disguised. As soon as Boulton became with Watt the sole owner of the steam engine patent, things moved rapidly. That was Boulton's way. At his request Watt dismantled the engine which had stood so long in the outbuilding at Kinneil, and shipped it—boiler, condenser, valves and pumps, four tons of machinery in all—by sea to Birmingham. He followed this with detailed plans and specifications for erecting the engine and for making certain improvements. It was arranged that as soon as his survey contract was completed, he would move to Birmingham where Boulton was to supply a house for him and his children. He would then supervise the erection of the engine and do whatever other work the firm needed at a salary of three hundred pounds a year.

He felt he was really beginning to see daylight. By April, 1774, he completed his survey and submitted it officially to Lord Cathcart, a prominent Member of Parliament from Glasgow. It was complete, including not only the usual measurements of mileage, depths of water, number of locks and costs of labor and land purchase, but also a careful comparison of the cost of transportation by the proposed canal with the various other methods used. It was his surveying swan song and he was proud of it.

A month later he took leave of Scotland forever and moved to Birmingham. The children stayed behind with Miss Macgregor and her family until he should be quite settled in his new environment.

His first problem was to assemble the engine. The workmanship was infinitely better than any he had seen at Carron, and the engine was quickly erected. He made two major changes. The cylinder was cast of solid grain tin, not hammered, and the condenser was made of a series of plates—inches apart and soldered. There were two air pumps. He checked and rechecked every part as it was added, and in November trial was made. The excellence of the workmanship proved its worth. There was practically no leakage and the strokes were swift and steady. Only two major changes seemed to be called for. Boulton felt that the cylinder should be of cast iron, and Watt saw signs that the plates of the condenser were about to come unsoldered and decided to return to the early method of injection of cold water.

As to the boring of a cast-iron cylinder, he pointed out the difficulties he had met with in getting the boring truly round and truly vertical. Boulton stuck to his point, however, and consulted John Wilkinson, an expert iron founder in the town of Chester. Wilkinson made use of a wholly new method of boring which he had devised himself. In his machine there was a straight central bar of great strength in the central axis of the cylinder. The cutting or boring instrument was made to slide along this bar as though it were a ruler, making the resulting cylinder perfectly straight in length and quite even in diameter throughout. Another problem solved.

Although the trial at Soho showed much greater promise than any made at Carron, it was obvious that between many necessary minor improvements and the actual time consumed in making even one engine, there would be a long period. Six years of the patent had already passed and both Watt and Boulton felt that an extension of the patent for at least twenty-five years was essential.

There were other factors that stirred the two men to such action. Unscrupulous people were trying to evade the patent and produce engines on his general principles. A man named Moore, a linen draper with no engineering experience, had already devised a plan for moving wheel carriages by steam. A man named Hatley who had at one time been employed at the Carron factory, copied and actually sold the plans of the Kinneil engine. Watt was less disturbed than his friend, still insisting that if Moore moved a wheeled carriage by steam he would have to use the engine that he had already patented. Everything, however, pointed to the need for a patent extension and with this in mind, he went to London, consulted Mr. Rous, his attorney, and decided to apply for an act for its extension at the next session of Parliament.

Routine was attended to and on February 28, 1775, a bill was introduced in Parliament to give to James Watt the sole rights to manufacture and sell the new type of steam engine according to the patent of 1769 extended for twenty-five years to 1800.

Watt had been to Parliament before when he secured his first patent, and he had been disgusted with what he called "the wrongheaded thinkers." He knew there would be opposition to his request, but the violence of those who claimed that a patent was a monopoly rose in the next few weeks to a white heat. The leader of the opposition was a surprise to him. Watt knew that the mining

interests were opposed to any one man having a monopoly on the steam engine. Their very lives depended
upon their ability to dig deeper and deeper into the
ground for coal and copper and tin, and the key to success was an engine to pump out the water. They wanted
to have their cake and eat it too. Watt knew this, but
when Edmund Burke, the Irish member for Bristol, took
up the cudgels against him, his heart sank.

Ever since his first speech back in 1766, Burke had
been a featured actor on the floor of Parliament. He was
the leader of the opposition to George III's American
policy, and to be opposed by him was almost a sign of
failure. Watt watched Burke as he strode up and down
between the benches; he watched the admiring glances
and nods of approval as the fiery little Irishman made
some particularly telling point, driving it home with
dramatic gestures. Was the whole world of steam, the
creation of his own imagination, to be suddenly smashed
to bits by one man's eloquence? He knew, of course, that
Burke spoke largely for the mining interests of Bristol.
As their representative he could do no less, but how generally his words would be accepted was Watt's worry.
His heart beat fast as he listened.

"Monopoly," Burke spelled out, "is the power, in one
man, of exclusive dealing in a commodity which others
might supply if not prevented by that power. This is
contrary to natural right. Monopoly should be granted
only for the good of the whole and not on arbitrary principles, and never for perpetuity."

Watt's ambition was to help the industrial world. Certainly, he thought, that was for the good of the whole. Everyone would benefit by an increase in industry.

For an hour Burke held forth. The claimant in the act, he pointed out, already possessed a monopoly for fourteen years, and he now was trying to increase it to thirty-eight. "I know not," he said, "how long this claimant expects to live, but I maintain that if we eliminate the years of childhood and those of senile old age, thirty-eight years is very close to perpetuity in this man's life."

He finally sat down, and Mr. Rous, Watt's attorney, was given time to speak. There was none of the fire of Edmund Burke, but quietly and methodically Mr. Rous summed up the case for James Watt. He pointed out the years of frustration, the personal sacrifice, not only of money but of health in securing for mankind in general the benefits of the harnessing of steam for power. He noted how his client had contributed his time and talents to many important canal and dredging projects at great physical suffering to himself.

Watt watched the members of the House carefully, trying to note reactions of approval or disapproval as Rous spoke. In their hands lay the fate of his nine years of dreaming and contriving. At times like this he missed Maggie. At the time the original patent was being considered, he remembered her saying, "Don't wear yourself out wi' worryin', Jamie. If the engine comes to naught, ye can do something else."

His attorney sat down, certain formalities were attended to, and the matter was left in the hands of the House of Commons to consider in private. How long he would have to wait he had no way of knowing. Parliament was much concerned at the moment with the future of the American colonies. It would, he knew, be a painful period of suspense.

Finally, on the 8th of May of the same year, 1775, Watt was happy to be able to write his father:

Dear Father,

After a series of various and violent opposition, I have at last got an Act of Parliament vesting the property of my new fire engine in me and my assigns throughout Great Britain and the Plantations, for twenty-five years to come, which I hope will be very beneficial to me, as there is already considerable demand for them.

I shall be obliged to stay here a few days longer, after which I return to Birmingham to set about making some engines that are ordered; after which I intend to give myself the happiness of seeing you and the dear children.

Ever your affectionate and dutiful son

James Watt

The only cloud on the horizon, after the success of his appeal, was the death of Dr. Small in Birmingham during the Parliamentary sessions. It was a bitter blow, for Dr. Small had been his counselor and friend, and being something of an inventor, the two found a multitude of common interests.

It had been agreed that should the patent be extended, Boulton and Watt would definitely become partners. Watt stayed in London long enough to have the proper legal steps taken, and then returned to Birmingham, a member of the new firm of Boulton and Watt. The terms were simple. Two thirds of any profits would go to Boulton who was to pay all expenses and keep the company books. Watt was to make all the drawings, give directions and make surveys.

Two definite jobs awaited him. The Bloomfield collieries in Staffordshire and Mr. Wilkinson's factory at Bradley in Shropshire had commissioned the firm to build engines for them. The Bloomfield engine was to be large with a fifty-inch cylinder, while the one for Bradley was slightly smaller. It was encouraging, and although he had in his mind several improvements, the engine at the moment was so far superior to the Newcomen that it could be considered successful.

The boring of the cylinder was a vital part of the whole, and John Wilkinson with his new method was given the contract. Roebuck's old Carron works put in a bid which Watt, with a little twinge of conscience, had to reject.

While the parts for these two first engines were being assembled he went, as he had promised, to see his father in Glasgow. He had said in his letter that he wanted to see him and the dear children. What he didn't say in his letter was that there was a third reason for his visit to Glasgow. That reason was Anne Macgregor. She had been watching over the children ever since the sad event of 1773. During these three years she had grown very fond of Margaret and Jemmy, and on the infrequent visits which Watt made to Glasgow Anne and he had become very fond of each other. With the engines in production and his permanent home to be in Birmingham, he made up his mind that he wanted to marry Anne Macgregor.

It wasn't, however, as simple as that. There was no question that she wanted to marry him, but she was a dutiful daughter and duly consulted her father. Mr. Macgregor was a linen draper and a very successful man of business, and to him marriage had a definite business side to it. When his daughter had first mentioned the possibility he had inquired, with a true Scot's thoroughness, into the financial prospects of this James Watt. Since at that time Watt himself was uncertain, parental agreement was withheld.

Now that the partnership was definite, the patent properly extended and orders actually coming in, Watt felt that the iron was hot enough to strike. Then one of his weaknesses overcame him. He was almost totally unable to bargain about finances. He had forced himself to do it during the period of his surveying, however badly it was done, because there was nothing else to do. When, however, Anne MacGregor became part of the deal, he found himself much too weak to even contemplate striking a bargain.

He asked Matthew Boulton if he would go with him to Glasgow and act as spokesman. Boulton was an excellent businessman but he felt this was a little out of his province and politely declined. He did, however, write a letter in which he placed a certain minimum valuation on Watt's new connection with him, and expressed such unqualified confidence in the engine that linen draper Macgregor was quite won over, and on July 29, 1776, James Watt and Anne Macgregor were married.

TWELVE

ANNE AND JAMES MOVED INTO THE HOUSE IN BIRMINGHAM supplied by Matthew Boulton. It was a large, plain brick house at Harper's Hill not far from the Soho works, surrounded by fields and gardens. Family life began again for Watt. Anne loved Margaret and Jemmy. She was proud of James and his ambition and encouraged him to devote all his time to it and leave the care of the household to her. She was an excellent housekeeper and a devoted wife, and Watt was once more able to focus his whole mind on inventing, and planning for the perfecting of his engine.

His first step was to set up a workshop in one of the upper rooms of the house where he could work without the distraction of ordinary household affairs. He avoided using space in the factory, which Boulton urged him to do, not only because it was noisy but because he knew he would be constantly called away to advise or inspect.

The improvements he contemplated, such as the use of steam expansively, the double-action engine, a new regulator and gauges, all required a great deal of theoretical working out on paper before any models could be made, and this work must be done in the undisturbed quiet of his own workshop.

Meanwhile, at the Soho factory there was great activity. Ever since he had first watched the skill with which Boulton's men worked, he had anticipated great things if he could get that skill to work on his engine. His ambition was being realized and he watched and guided the work with a new enthusiasm.

He still felt very strongly that a rotatory engine was an essential factor in the use of steam. A circular motion was more useful than the up and down for anything except pumping. But at the moment, the crisis in the mines all over England and Wales demanded the pump, and that must have priority.

He watched carefully as the old Kinneil engine was set up, and made many changes for the better. An inch thick, eighteen-inch cylinder weighing one thousand pounds was very accurately cast by John Wilkinson. The iron piston was surrounded by a brass hoop two inches broad to diminish friction. It was made tight by the use of papier-mâché, grease, black lead, and oil which was drained through an old hat, to lubricate the sides. An iron weight was placed above to prevent the piston from leaving the papier-mâché behind in its stroke.

Many adjustments had to be made, but after a month of experimenting, the engine was doing two thousand strokes on only one hundredweight of coal, an unusual economy of fuel. When it was finally set up, it was exhibited not only to prospective buyers, but was used to pump water for the factory's water wheels. The men nicknamed it "Beelzebub" and grew to look upon it with real admiration.

Watt felt that his troubles were over. Here was "Beelzebub" helping to turn the wheels of industry and actually earning its keep as the first condensing steam engine in the world. There was a definite need for his steam engine. George III in London was fighting a war with the American colonists. He desperately needed cannon and any number of other war products, and coal was now commonly used in the smelting of iron ore. The coal miners were hard pressed and needed engines to pump out the water as the shafts grew deeper under the crisis demand. Watt's engine was the answer.

A few months before he and Anne were married, the firm received an order for an engine from the Bloomfield collieries. They were only a short distance from Birmingham and it was easy for him to supervise the construction of an engine there, and the results were even better than he and Boulton had anticipated.

The engine with a fifty-inch cylinder, and a stroke of seven feet worked a pump fourteen and a quarter inches in diameter on a quarter of the fuel required by the common engine. The ninety-foot pit had fifty-seven feet of water in it and at fourteen to fifteen strokes a minute the engine and pump emptied it in less than an hour. Cheers rose from the crowd as the last drop of water was pumped out.

Birmingham was enthusiastic, and Watt read with pride the account in the local *Gazette:*

March 11, 1776—On Friday last a Steam Engine constructed on Mr. Watt's new Principles was set to work at the Bloomfield Colliery near Dudley in the presence of a number of Scientific Gentlemen whose Curiosity was excited to see the first Movements of so singular and so powerful a machine; and whose Expectations were fully gratified by the Excellence of its Performance.

The liberal spirit shown by the Proprietors of Bloomfield in ordering this, the first large engine of the kind that hath ever been made, and in rejecting a common one which they had begun to erect, entitle them to the Thanks of the Public, for by this example the Doubts of the Inexperienced are dispelled and the Importance and Usefulness of the Invention is finally decided.

With this success what possible difficulty could there be now? This he was soon to find out. It was one thing to build a single engine under his own guidance, using the most skilled men in the factory. But as news of the Act of Parliament, which obviously recognized the superior quality of Watt's invention, spread from factory to factory and mine to mine, inquiries began coming in. Should there be increased orders, more and more skilled mechanics would be needed, and they just didn't exist. This was a real problem.

To his surprise, the man who pointed this out to him and looked upon it as insurmountable was John Smeaton, the engineer and his competitor in much of his surveying work. Smeaton had won the contract for the Lomond Passage in 1767 and Watt had underbid him in many

other contracts. It was a friendly rivalry, and Smeaton
had always expressed interest and faith in his engine.

"Ye've got an idea, Mr. Watt," he said many times,
"but it's too complicated. There are not enough men in
all of England skillful enough to build it in any quantity."

This was a personal opinion and Watt went so far as to
agree that skilled mechanics were lacking, but insisted
that he could train them. However, when a distiller in
Stratford-le-Bow near London ordered an engine to
pump fifteen thousand gallons of ale per hour to a height
of sixty feet and Smeaton announced publicly that it
wouldn't work, Watt felt he had gone too far. Smeaton
wrote in the name of the Society of Engineers which
gave his opinion a particular weight.

Adverse comment was just what the firm didn't want,
and the Bow engine became rather a test case. An
engine had already been built for John Wilkinson, the
iron founder, who used it to blow his bellows. It had
been called the Willy engine, and on its success or failure
hung the beginning of a reputation. It was eagerly
watched by friend and critic alike and its success was
unquestionable. Watt had supervised every step. The
parts were made and assembled by the best workmen in
the Soho plant. The same care must be used in the case
of the Bow engine. He must go to London to see personally to the assembling of the parts which were already
on the way.

Unfortunately, stress of work at the Soho plant delayed
his London trip and by the time he arrived the worst had
happened. The engine had been assembled and tried in

the presence of a large crowd. It stopped after a few strokes and no amount of tinkering would make it budge. The Society of Engineers must be right, the audience agreed, and when Watt appeared, many of them told him so.

He was not convinced, and made a careful check of the engine. He found it most inexpertly put together, and he noted that it was being driven up to sixteen strokes a minute when it had been regulated for only ten. This would have been hard to understand if he hadn't found that the engineer who was responsible for running the engine had been sampling his employer's ale a little too freely and consequently laying a too heavy hand on the steam supply. With a few mechanical and one human alteration the engine performed most satisfactorily, but it had been a close call. Watt was determined that from then on, every engine must be supervised by himself.

Orders were being considered from all over England, which meant a great deal of traveling about if he were to do this, but as it took about three weeks to assemble the parts for an engine, it was not impossible. John Wilkinson was commissioned to provide cylinders of various sizes, from twelve to fifty inches, and condensers to suit. These were kept at Soho to be ready for production.

In spite of Smeaton and the Society of Engineers, public opinion seemed satisfied with the success of the Willy, Bloomfield and Bow engines and further orders began coming in. Two other London distillers ordered engines. Tin mines at Truro in Cornwall and as far west as Wales sent desperate requests for help. They were losing money and would have to shut down if Mr. Watt couldn't save them.

In the midst of all this, Jamie received a very official letter from Russia offering him a position under the Imperial Government at a yearly salary of a thousand pounds. A few years before he had been told by his friend Robison that he might be useful in Russia, but this time it was a definite offer. The money was a great temptation, and Watt looked back on the dark days when he might easily have accepted it, but things were different now. He owed a definite loyalty to Matthew Boulton; by his surveying work he had paid off most of his debts, and he was about to realize the success of a dream. All doubt about his decision faded when he had a letter from his friend Dr. Darwin, who wrote:

> Lord, how frightened I was when I heard a Russian bear had laid hold of you with his great paw, and was dragging you to Russia. Pray don't go if you can help it. Russia is like the den of Cacua; you see the footsteps of many beasts going thither, but of few returning. I hope your fire engine will keep you here.
>
> Your loyal friend
> Erasmus Darwin

Watt was really dedicated to his engine. He knew in his heart that no offer would take him permanently away from England, but he was glad that his old friend felt so strongly about it.

He tried to solve the problem of skilled mechanics by

personally instructing the most promising of the workmen and encouraging them with increased pay as they demonstrated their care and skill. New men were constantly applying, but the number of possible workers was pitifully small.

Then one day when Watt was sitting with Boulton in the office, an applicant named William Murdock was shown in. He stood, almost apologetically, in front of the two partners in spite of his size and obvious physical strength. The routine questions were asked and answered. He was twenty-two years old and had been born in Ayrshire. He had always been interested in mechanics and had trained himself in the art. He had had no experience with steam engines, though he was familiar with the working of the Newcomen atmospheric engine.

The questioning over, he stood rather nervously twisting his hat in his hand which drew Watt's attention to it, and to relieve this young man's evident nervousness, he spoke of it.

"That is rather an unusual hat, Mr. Murdock," he commented.

Murdock smiled faintly. "I guess you might say so, Mr. Watt," he answered. "I turned it out myself on a wee lathe. It's all right if it doesn't get too wet."

Watt looked at Mr. Boulton who nodded. The same thought occurred to them both. Any man who had the imagination to think of a wooden hat and the skill to produce one would certainly be useful in the Soho plant. William Murdock was hired at once at fifteen shillings a week. Inside of a week he had grasped the principles of the Watt engine and demonstrated an unusual skill in putting together the various parts. He was a find, and when the parts for the first engine for a Cornish tin mine at Truro were ready to be shipped, Watt took Murdock along with him to supervise the assembling.

The two men naturally expected to be received with some show of welcome, very like re-enforcements arriving at the scene of a losing battle, but they had not reckoned with the ignorance that accompanied poverty. Truro was about two hundred miles from Birmingham on an inlet of the east coast. The surrounding country was desolate save for stunted bushes and an occasional tree. The roads, if they could be called that, were rutted and muddy and went straight and steep down the sides of the hills so that their horses constantly slipped and frequently fell. Poverty and dirt were everywhere and both men shuddered at the thought of spending any length of time in such a place.

When they reached the pit head their spirits went even lower. Around the openings in the ground, the earth was piled in muddy mountains from which water oozed. Mud was everywhere: muddy carts, muddy horses and muddy men.

The men were ignorant. They were sullen in an instinctive attempt to conceal their ignorance. The mine owners were in London and the so-called "captains" who were in charge seemed as dull-witted as their men. Watt examined the Newcomen engine which he was to replace with his own. It was working feebly, but it was obvious that as the digging went deeper, it would prove quite inadequate against the rising water.

The day after he and Murdock arrived, wagons brought the parts of his engine to the pit head. Picking a dozen of the most promising-looking men, Watt started construction. The first step was the building of a suitable platform. This proved not to be too difficult, but when he began the actual assembling of the parts, Watt was met by an unexpected obstacle. He and Murdock would carefully explain the necessary construction and points of some part, and then, whether from ignorance or spite, the men would make the most clumsy mistakes and the work would have to be done over several times.

It got so bad that Watt called the three captains into the ramshackle building that served as an office and protested. This was the part of the work that he knew he was not fitted for, but it had to be done.

"You gentlemen know, of course," he began, "that we are here at the request of your owners to replace your old engine with one of our design?"

The captains nodded rather stiffly, but said nothing. He drew a deep breath and went on. "It is impossible for us to erect our engine without the help of your men. Our instructions are simple, and yet nothing is done right."

A stolid, Cornish stare was the only response. He continued, "All this takes valuable time and if any parts are broken, we may have to send back to Birmingham for replacements—more time lost. Is there nothing you gentlemen can do to make the men understand?" He used the word "gentlemen" very reluctantly, but diplomacy demanded it. The captains shrugged their shoulders.

"Why do you shrug your shoulders?" He asked. "The owners are in London and you are in charge. Surely—"

One of the captains interrupted him. "The thing is too complicated," he said, "and it's no better than the old one."

Watt saw a point of argument. "How do you know that until you try it?" he asked.

"You'll have to pay the men more money if you want to build it," said the captain.

"But I have no authority to pay more," Watt protested. He was beginning to feel rather terrifyingly frustrated. There was a fluttering in his stomach.

The shoulders again shrugged. There was a pause and Watt looked frantically at Murdock who sensed the despair in his companion's glance. He leaned over to Watt and said in a half whisper, "Leave 'em to me, laddie." Watt wondered what possible further arguments Murdock could offer, but he was totally unprepared for what followed.

Murdock rose to his feet, stepped to the door and locked it. He then took off his shirt, strode over and stood in front of the three captains.

"We'll pay no more wages, but ye'll build the engine," he said in a tone of complete finality.

"But I—we—" one of the captains started to protest. Murdock clenched his fists and there was a ripple of muscles up to his powerful shoulders.

"I think ye heard me?" he said questioningly.

One of the captains shook his head, rose and started for the door. He got no farther than two steps when Murdock's fist caught him on the jaw. Whirling around, he crumpled against the wall. One of his companions uttered a protest which was met with the same answer, and Murdock stood towering over the third captain.

"Will ye build the engine?" he asked. With one look at this wild man from Birmingham, who spoke the only language for ending arguments known around the pits, the terrified man agreed.

The engine was built.

The ignorant and critical stood around the pit head and watched the first test. The water, they claimed, was the heaviest in the whole county and no engine could "fork" it, which was their expression for pumping. Watt had the engine run at its fullest possible power. The noise was terrific and that seemed to impress everyone, but the important thing was that the water level in the depth of the mine became lower and lower. Even the ignorant and the critical were heard to remark that this new engine "could fork anything."

After several weeks in Cornwall, Watt was glad to get home to Birmingham. He had acquired not only a greater respect for William Murdock, but also a fine feeling of friendship such as develops when two men work and suffer together. He insisted upon an increase in salary for him, and from then on he looked upon him as his right-hand man, one who would make possible the ultimate success of his engine. He turned over to him the training of a force of new men who would be able to construct with real accuracy the increasing number of engines which the Soho factory was being called upon to produce.

George III with a stubborn single-mindedness wanted coal and tin for his war effort against the American colonies. The ordinary British citizen wanted coal for the simple purpose of living. The coal and tin producers were all losing money as the expense of draining their mines to meet the new demand rose to a quarter of a million pounds in three years. It was a desperate situation for all of England, and Watt realized only too well that perfecting and producing his engine in quantity was the only solution.

THIRTEEN

WITH WILLIAM MURDOCK SUPERVISING THE WORK AT Soho, and Mr. Boulton taking care of orders, Watt set to work on the improvements to his engine that lack of time had prevented him from perfecting.

He had felt from the start that merely doing the work was not the only purpose of the engine. That work must be done economically, which meant that as little fuel as possible must be used. The separate condenser had been the first step in this direction. Now, he told himself, he must devise some way of making use of the magic power of steam to expand. In other words, he must see that fuel was saved by using less steam to do the same amount of work. He had had for some time a pretty clear picture in his mind of the theory of how this could be done. This theory must be brought down to cold fact before any real use could be made of it.

It was obvious to him that if the steam from the boiler were cut off at some point in the cylinder, its power of expanding would carry the piston the rest of the way.

135

There was, however, a difficulty here that must be cleared up. At just what point should the steam be cut off? He knew that the pressure of the expanding steam would not be as great as though the full force of a cylinder full of steam had been used. He must find the point of greatest efficiency.

To answer this question he built a small model cylinder and piston. He then devised a mechanical attachment to the cylinder which gave an automatic recording of the diminishing pressure of the steam on a sheet of paper fitted to a revolving drum and actuated directly by the steam pressure in the cylinder. From a study of the resulting diagram he determined that if the steam were cut off, after a quarter stroke, the effect would be equal to more than half the effect that would have been produced had steam been admitted into the cylinder for the full stroke. Here, then, three fourths of the steam would be saved at the loss of less than half the working effect, a real saving in fuel.

While this was most satisfactory, it occurred to Jamie that there should be some unit of measurement to indicate in engines of varying sizes just what their working effect was. Work done, he told himself, was really resistance overcome—or the application of force through distance against resistance. Work was done so universally by horses that he wondered why his engine could not in some way be compared to the work done by a horse.

He remembered that in 1702 Savery had compared the work done by one of his engines to the same work accomplished by a group of horses working in shifts. This was rather vague and Watt decided to see if he could determine how much work one horse would do in one minute. He made innumerable experiments with horses pulling weights over pulleys, and finally determined that one good dray horse could in one minute raise a total of thirty-three thousand pounds one foot off the ground. This he called a "horsepower."

Then, by means of an indicator attached to the cylinder, he determined the amount of exhaustion in the cylinder at any given point. He realized that it was only necessary to know the length of stroke, and to indicate the pressure of the steam upon the piston exerted during each instant of its movement to obtain the factors of the work done by each stroke. This could then be easily compared to the work done in one minute by one horse. He began speaking of different-sized engines as being of varying horsepower and the term met with general approval.

The problem of how to make his engine produce a rotative or circular motion had been in his mind from the first. It was not only the movement used in all mills, but was essential if any wagons or carriages were to be moved by steam. Even his spiral oar or screw propeller, which he had suggested to Dr. Small in 1772, as a means of propelling barges on the canals depended upon a circular motion. Up to now the desperate cry all over England was for pumping engines. They were an economic necessity if the coal mines were to stay in business at all. Water wheels still turned the machinery for mills and for the moment mill owners were satisfied, but Jamie went right on inventing.

The crank of a foot lathe had first occurred to him as the obvious method. When this was stolen from him by Cartwright, he had consoled himself with the thought that it was not really a patentable idea. The steam wheel had been his next thought, but this, while quite sound in theory, was far too complicated to put to any practical use. He felt sure that the ultimate way to secure a circular motion would be by some simple use of the up-and-down movement of his pumping engine.

With this thought in mind he consulted with William Murdock who had become invaluable to him for his technical skill and his imagination. Together they covered pages with crude drawings, and put together hastily built models to prove or disprove some mechanical point. After they had discarded three or four methods, Murdock suggested that possibly if they substituted wheels for the treadle action of the lathe they would have an answer. More pictures were drawn, and finally an idea evolved.

There would be the central or working wheel toothed and fixed to a shaft carrying a fly. The connecting rod of the working beam of his pumping engine would carry a wheel on a fixed axis; this to be always in contact with the working wheel. By the reaction of the engine this wheel would go around the working wheel, turning it twice for every stroke of the engine.

Since this device consisted of one round object going around another, Watt named it the sun and planet method. It was simple and practical, and since it had the advantage of turning the working wheel twice for every stroke of the engine, it was economical. Murdock made a model of it and they planned to use it in a full-scale engine as soon as possible.

The Newcomen engine had been what was called an atmospheric engine. That is, the working power was achieved by the weight of the atmosphere forcing the piston down into a vacuum. Watt had altered this and produced a *real* steam engine by closing the top of the cylinder and surrounding the piston with a case of steam which served instead of the atmosphere to break the equilibrium and force down the piston.

It occurred to Watt that since steam, used either whole or expansively, drove the piston up, it might just as well be used to drive it down and not merely to break the equilibrium. This would create a double-action engine with usable power in each stroke.

To accomplish this he built a model engine in which pipes led from the boiler to points both above and below this piston. Also, there were valves on both sides of the piston to alternately evacuate the steam from whichever side it was desired to establish a vacuum. It was still a condensing engine, the vacuum assisting the steam in whichever direction the piston was to be driven.

His two main goals had always been the greatest power and the lowest consumption of fuel. The separate condenser and the use of steam expansively had pretty well achieved this latter. The double-action engine added power. Then he decided to go a step further. There was no way of knowing what heavy machinery might be introduced into the expanding industry of England and he wanted to be prepared.

This led him naturally to the thought of a double engine. This would consist of two engines, a primary and a secondary. The steam vessels and condensers would be connected by pipes and valves so that they could be worked either independently or together, and make the strokes either alternately or at the same time, whichever was required.

He was in his element. His mind was teeming with ideas for a more efficient harnessing and controlling of the magic force of steam. His work was interrupted from time to time by his prolonged trips to Cornwall or Wales or other parts of England to supervise the erection of new engines, and by his sick headaches which still plagued him.

These often drove him to say to Anne that he would give up this foolish inventing business. Anne knew only too well that he would never give it up, but she was secretly glad for the days when he stayed at home and really enjoyed his growing family. In 1777 his second son Gregory had been born, and in 1779 his daughter Jessie. Jemmy, at the age of fifteen, was working for Mr. Wilkinson and proving himself quite worthy of his ingenious father. At home were Margaret, Maggie's daughter, and Anne's two children, Gregory, aged five, and Jessie, two years younger.

Little Jessie was a sweet child, but unhappily she seemed to have the inherited weakness, and Anne and

Jamie were fearful for her life. Gregory was his joy and he planned great things for him and Jemmy. "They'll take over when I'm too old to work," he always told Anne. In his workshop he delighted in making toys or repairing dolls as he had done for Maggie and his little brother John in the old days.

Even when he was working, Jamie gave up one evening a month to attending meetings of a group of men who called themselves the "Lunar Society." They met at each other's houses at the full of the moon in order to be able to walk home without running the risk of attack in the dark streets. On moving to Birmingham Jamie had been urged by Matthew Boulton to join the newly formed group, and he had become an enthusiastic member.

The Lunar Society was made up of men well known in the field of natural philosophy. Each one in his own specialty had contributed to the growing knowledge of Nature and her mysteries. There were such men as Erasmus Darwin, the great physician and botanist; William Herschel, astronomer and musician, who had just announced his discovery of a new planet in the sky which he named Uranus; Josiah Wedgwood, who was fast building up a great pottery industry and had recently presented a dinner service to Catherine II of Russia; and John Smeaton, James's former rival in the surveying field.

The talk at the meetings naturally covered a wide field of subjects, and after a few months the other members began to realize that James Watt was able to talk brilliantly on any segment of this general field, and offer most original approaches to any problem.

One evening in 1780 as they were walking home together after a meeting, Dr. Darwin, knowing Watt's love for inventions, told him of something he had devised. He called it a "bigrapher" and it consisted of a second quill attached by an arm to the one in use, which made a copy of whatever was being written. He was quite enthusiastic about the idea, but admitted that in practice it was a little clumsy and he hadn't tried to patent it.

Watt was interested for a very practical reason. All the records of his company had to be copied laboriously by hand. As business increased, the correspondence and records of the firm became a real problem. The copying of so many letters became a great hardship and time waster. Dr. Darwin's bigrapher set him to thinking of some better method of duplicating copies. He thought about it all that night, and in a few days he wrote to his friend Darwin.

—I have fallen on a way of copying writing chemically, which beats your bigrapher hollow. I can copy a whole sheet letter in five minutes. I send a copy of the other page enclosed for your conviction, and I tell you further that I can do still better than that copy.

The first thought that had occurred to him was simply to force the ink through the paper so it would appear on the other side. Then he found a better result if he moistened the paper with an astringent. For months he worked on the problem of finding a suitable ink which would give a clear copy without damaging the original. When he had settled on this he realized that to prepare a sheet for copying with the right astringent and the proper ink took so much time that it defeated the whole purpose of making quick copies.

Then he hit on the notion of preparing a large quantity of the paper at one time and keeping it for use when needed. He did this by means of what he called "damping boxes" made of wood, lined with tin foil or sheet lead with a lid fitting close to the interior of the sides, to allow either a small or large quantity of copying paper to be damped at one time. He found he could keep this paper moist by keeping the leaves between boards of wainscot, with tin foil next to the paper an inch or so beyond in order to fold over. In this way any amount of paper could be kept in instant readiness for as long as a month.

In May of 1780 he received a patent for his "new method of copying letters and other writings expeditiously," as it was officially described. Having invented it, he turned it over to Mr. Boulton and Mr. Keir, the chemist and a member of the Lunar Society. He left it up to them to manufacture and distribute.

Discussions at the meetings of the Lunar Society often took his mind off his engine. He couldn't seem to resist following through with any new idea that was suggested. "I've started a new hare," was one of his favorite expressions. No sooner had he perfected the copying machine idea, suggested by Dr. Darwin, and gone back to his engine than he was sidetracked again.

This time it was Dr. Joseph Priestley who put an idea in his head. Dr. Priestley was the most recent member of the Lunar Society, having only just moved to Birmingham. He was famous, among other things, for his discovery in 1774 of oxygen, which he called "dephlogisticated air." He used this term as he was a firm believer in the existence of a substance called phlogiston or fire element. Priestley's wife's brother was iron founder for Boulton and Watt, and he and Watt drew rather naturally together.

One evening early in 1783 Dr. Priestley was telling the assembled members of an experiment he had just made which had rather peculiar results.

"You gentlemen may remember," he said, "how about two years ago Mr. Warltire, the chemist, passed a spark through a mixture of common air and inflammable air in a closed metal flask to determine whether heat was heavy or not. When the spark passed through there was a loud explosion and the two airs seemed to have disappeared."

There were nods of interest followed by a silence of expectancy to hear what experiment the ingenious Dr. Priestley might have made.

"It occurred to me," he continued, "that nothing ever completely disappears, and that there must be some residue. I repeated Warltire's experiment with one difference. I used a glass vessel instead of a metal one, so that I could see any change that might take place during or after the explosion. To my surprise I noted that whereas the glass vessel was quite clear before the explosion, when it cooled off there were drops of clear liquid on the sides. This was strange, but stranger still was the fact that the weight of this liquid, which was pure water, was the same as the weight of the two gases I had introduced."

There were expressions of surprise and some desultory discussion, but being late, with the moon still bright, the meeting broke up.

That night Watt lay awake thinking. The last words that Priestley had used somehow haunted him, "the weight of the water was the same as the weight of the two gases." A problem of any sort was a challenge. The next morning he set up apparatus similar to what Priestley had used and conducted the same experiment. Sure enough, the gases were replaced by drops of water. His mind began its usual far-reaching analysis of the situation.

The gases had disappeared and water had appeared. Why wasn't it possible that water was not the single element everyone thought it to be? Why couldn't it be a combination of these two gases? He tried the gases in different combinations. He found that when he used twice as much inflammable air as he did the oxygen, or dephlogisticated air, nothing was left but the water.

Watt was now the logical scientist. It must be, he reasoned, that water, which from ancient times had been looked upon as a single element, was in reality composed of two parts of inflammable air and one part of the oxygen that Priestley had discovered. The thought gave him almost the same thrill he had felt when the idea of a separate condenser sprang into his mind.

On April 23, 1783, he wrote to Dr. Priestley who had gone to London to attend a meeting of the Royal Society, explained his findings and asked him to have his letter read at the meeting, thus giving his discovery the advantage of a public hearing. Dr. Banks, the president of the Royal Society, read the letter privately and suggested to Priestley that the public reading be delayed as the conclusions were altogether too bold. Dr. Priestley suggested to Watt that perhaps he had better review his findings, but that the letter would be placed on file anyway.

Watt reviewed his findings with the same result, and so informed Priestley. Water was, he was still convinced, composed of two parts of inflammable air and one part of oxygen, and he was quite willing to back the theory against all comers. This became necessary sooner than he thought. In January, 1784, he received the news that Sir Henry Cavendish, a wealthy amateur chemist, had read a paper before the Royal Society outlining the same theory in almost identical terms. As if this were not bad enough, the great French chemist, Antoine Lavoisier, claimed to have made similar experiments.

Finally, a year later, in April, 1784, Watt's letter was publicly read and the date, a year earlier, noted. The question of priority of discovery was brought up. There were supporters of all three, but the date of Watt's original letter and its positive findings were accepted by the Society as sufficient proof. The next year he was elected a Fellow of the Royal Society. The honor delighted him, but the arguments pro and con had annoyed him. He felt that it was really unimportant who discovered the composition of water. The important thing was that it was discovered. His steam engine was still the first thing in his life.

FOURTEEN

Since the general acceptance of the Watt engine, the production of iron in England had more than doubled. The coal mines were more productive, and consequently there was more coke for the process of smelting. John Wilkinson, the iron founder, had for some time been convinced that iron that was heated and hammered had a much greater toughness than iron that was cast. He put it up to Watt to produce an engine that would raise a stamp or tilt hammer of fifteen hundred pounds thirty or forty times a minute.

Watt was always glad of any chance to use his engine for purposes other than pumping water. Furthermore, the speed with which the tilt hammer must work called for the use of his rotary engine. This could be a public demonstration of it. If it worked here there was nothing to prevent its working in textile mills or flour mills. He set to work with great enthusiasm. If successful, he told Boulton, there should be great demand for what he called "these battering-rams."

His first experiment was with a hammer of only sixty pounds. He soon found that the chief problems were the relations between the weight of the hammer, the height above the iron to be forged, and the number of blows that could be struck in a minute. The human elements had to be brought into his calculations also, because there was a physical limit to the number of pieces of iron that the workmen could handle in a minute. The machine had to be geared to this figure.

Watt tried with hammers weighing from one hundred and fifty to a thousand pounds. He found that by diminishing the height of the hammer over the iron he could get blows of two hundred and fifty to three hundred per minute which was more than anyone had thought possible. This unfortunately proved not only too fast for the proper handling of the hot iron, but too powerful for the iron itself which was knocked to pieces. He finally settled on twenty engine strokes a minute with a thousand-pound hammer falling from a height of two feet at a rate of ninety blows per minute. This seemed to answer the purpose.

This was success with a tilt hammer. His rotary engine had worked well in an iron foundry. Would it work equally well in wool, cotton or grist mills? The wool and cotton mills were equipped with machines such as Hargreaves' jenny, Cartwright's frame, and Crompton's "mule" which was a combination of the jenny and the frame. These were in most instances run by water power, though horses and mules were still used. Why not steam?

Boulton approached several mill owners, but they

scoffed at the idea. Wind, water and horses had served them for a generation. Why sink money into some complicated bit of mechanism which they couldn't or wouldn't understand? Boulton was not one to be easily discouraged. He went to London and consulted with several moneylenders. Would they advance money to build a grist mill equipped with grindstones, turned by steam? The unanimous answer was "no." It was a preposterous idea. It would cost thousands of pounds and would put out of business all the grist mills worked by horse or water power. More than this, it would bring idleness and poverty to hundreds of workers.

Watt was willing to take this answer and turn to other fields, but Matthew Boulton had unbounded faith in the engine. Among his friends, he raised a large sum of money and in 1783 he engaged Samuel Wyatt, a leading architect, to draw plans for the Albion Mills, a steam grist mill in Southwark at the end of Blackfriars Bridge.

To Watt fell the task of designing the engines. It was decided that there would be two double-acting rotary engines equipped with sun and planet mechanism. They were to be of fifty horsepower and capable of working twenty pairs of millstones. The idea was tremendous but risky. It was built entirely on Boulton's unquenchable optimism and the gambling instinct of a few friendly investors.

It would take several years to get the proposed mill into production, and meanwhile Watt still had the responsibility of supplying the mines of England with pumping engines. He still had to battle with the mine

owners about money due on his engines. He had to keep
an eye out for competitors, and all the time his mind was
filled with ideas for improvements in his own engine.

The Watt engine was being talked about, especially
the new rotary type, news of the Albion Mills naturally
having traveled through the coffee shops of London. To
most Londoners, it was merely an incomprehensible invention that served as gossip while sipping coffee or
drinking ale. In Windsor Castle there was a Londoner of
a different stamp. King George had always been interested in things mechanical. In fact, he had a reputation
as a repairer of watches, and he insisted upon seeing a
rotary engine at work. The Albion Mills not being completed, he compromised on a small rotary engine that
Boulton and Watt had installed on an experimental basis
in the brewery of a Mr. Whitehead on the outskirts of
London.

The brewery was small, and the glamour was out of
all proportion to it. The double line of red-coated King's
guards with their fur caps, the dressing up of the nearby
shops, the loads of chickens brought to neighborhood
inns to serve as the chief ingredient of the potpies
prepared for the expected crowds, and finally the ringing
of church bells and the appearance of the splendid royal
carriage—all suggested some world-shaking event.

To Watt the event was large if not world-shaking. The
King wanted to know about a rotary engine, and he was
to tell him. Royal interest was vital, and here it was. The
two dreamers were to meet at last.

George saw a stoop-shouldered man in his fifties,

simply dressed in black, possessing a rather sallow complexion, but a firm jaw and penetrating eyes, his hair unpowdered and cut in the prevailing fashion, bushing out on each side to the top of his high coat collar. Watt greeted his monarch, a fat, stolid, rather heavy-faced man slightly younger than himself with fair skin and very prominent blue eyes.

The King congratulated him on his ingenuity, asked most intelligent questions, expressed a desire to see him again and drove off in his royal carriage.

It was, of course, inevitable that the engine should be imitated. To the average coffeehouse patron it was a bit of magic that he didn't pretend to understand, but there were men in England with a smattering of scientific knowledge who were able to adapt Watt's principles to engines of their own making. These engines were not good. They puffed and wheezed—asthmatic, Watt called them. They lost power and refused to go more than twenty or thirty strokes without resting. Their only attraction to the mine owners was that they could be had at very low cost. The Cornish mines became arrogant. If Watt wouldn't reduce his prices then they would buy the competing engines.

Watt surprised himself on one occasion by walking out of a meeting after telling the mine owners that he was not going to dicker with anyone. If and when they wanted his engine they could come to Soho and buy it on his terms. This was courageous and in some cases this attitude produced results, but every contract in England seemed to involve disputes. The firm was not making money, but Watt knew that to stop producing engines would be the end of the business. For the moment, they would simply have to ignore the imitators and improve their own engine to its full potential.

Then Jacques Périer appeared and the problem became international. Périer was a member of a large and influential Paris family, prominent in industry and the professions. He had, through his influence, obtained the concession—which meant royal permission—to supply water to the city of Paris by pumping it from the Seine River and distributing it. To do the pumping he had been using a Newcomen engine. Then word of Watt's engine reached Paris and Périer made a hasty trip across the channel and visited Soho.

He was most politely received, and much impressed with what he saw; so much so, in fact, that when he returned to France he sent a gentleman named Betancourt back to Soho to observe. These observations were made with somewhat unscrupulous care for details, and included an attempt to bribe two or three workmen to go to Paris and build engines for the Périer Brothers.

Mr. Boulton, with his usual foresight, had secured from Louis XVI a writ entitling him to the exclusive manufacturing rights of the engine in France. This didn't appear to bother Périer who proceeded to build three engines. One was built under the name of Boulton and Watt quite legitimately, but the other two were built with what Périer naïvely spoke of as *"changements qu'il avoir imaginé."* M. Betancourt had done his observing very thoroughly, but Périer gave the credit to his own imagination.

Watt and Boulton made a hurried trip to Paris which annoyed Périer whose conscience wasn't any too clear. The two French-built engines refused to do more than two or three strokes a minute until Watt's expert hands put them to rights. The royal decree in favor of Boulton and Watt was upheld, and Périer had to be content with building a huge factory to produce engines under Watt's directions.

After this experience, Watt was afraid of any foreign contacts. There were no international patent laws, and there were ingenious and not too scrupulous men across the channel. Matthew Boulton, however, did not share Watt's fear and negotiated a contract in Holland. Watt had a feeling that his engine was slipping out of his grasp, and he must do something to protect himself. Between 1781 and 1784 he secured patents which in official words were "for certain new improvements upon fire or steam engines for raising water, and other mechanisms applicable to the same." The specifications covered the expansive use of steam, the double-acting engine, the double engine, the sun and planet method of securing rotary motion, and a method of moving wheeled vehicles. Officially, at least, he was safe from imitators.

This was one burden off his mind, but he was not through. He was not yet fully satisfied with his engine. All the piracies and plagiaries that had been practiced on him made him anxious to reach perfection, and further patent protection. After all, this was his dream, and before he was too old he wanted to realize it to the full.

Years before, he had discussed with his friend Robison the possibility of moving wheeled carriages by steam, and in 1778 he had suggested to Dr. Black what he called his spiral oar for moving barges on the canals. Both of these ideas had been passed over due to pressure of work on the actual engine itself.

With the fundamentals of his engine safely covered by patents, he began again to visualize the possible application of steam to chaises or canal barges. In the early 1780's he remembered that a linen draper named Moore had used steam to move carriages, but the engine he used was Watt's invention, and nothing much came of it. Watt included the specifications in his patent of 1784, although he felt it was very defective and did it only to keep other people from similar patents. The exact wording was "steam engines which are applied to give motion to wheel carriages for removing persons or goods from place to place."

William Murdock had already built what he called a locomotive engine along the lines laid down by Watt. He had driven it down the main street of his home town of Redruth amidst fire and steam, to the consternation of the local parson who was sitting in the parsonage garden when, as he put it later, "the Devil roared by." Watt looked unfavorably on this since he felt that Murdock was too valuable a man to be wasting his time on such impractical—even if sensational—experiments.

In spite of this, however, he carefully analyzed all the possibilities of a steam carriage. For the sake of lightness he planned that the outside of the boiler should be made of wood, strongly secured by hoops to prevent it from bursting. The fire was to be contained in a vessel of metal within the boiler and surrounded entirely by the water to be heated, except at the openings to admit air to the fire, to put in the fuel and to let out the smoke.

He would use his sun and planet rotatory engine, and because more power would be needed in climbing hills or on soft roads, he devised a series of notched wheels of different diameters which could be moved at will and attached to a fixed sprocket on the axle of the carriage. The carriage would be steered by altering the angle of inclination of its fore and hind wheels to one another by means of a lever.

He carefully figured out the length of stroke, the size and thickness of the cylinder and the boiler. The proper place for the engine, he decided, was behind the carriage to act on the hind wheels. He saw in the shaking of the carriage, when in motion on rough roads, the danger, not only of making the coals fall through the grate before being consumed, but also of loosening the joints of the cylinder. But he did point out to Mr. Boulton that this shaking made it unnecessary to plan a method of poking the fire.

The weight of the whole thing troubled him, and he sent Mr. Boulton an estimate of this in great detail.

A post chaise weighs about	1,000 lbs.
the boiler and water would weigh	660
the engine and wheels say	200
the fly, three feet in diameter, containing the power of one stroke of the engine	100
the organ pipe condenser, bellows	100
three persons including the driver	400
their luggage	200
Coals for four hours @ fifteen pounds per hour	60
Water for two hours	180
Total	2,900

"The whole matter," he added in his letter, "seems to turn on an answer to the question of whether eighty pounds be sufficient power to remove a post chaise on a tolerably good and level road at the rate of four miles in an hour."

To Watt, even after his careful analysis of possibilities, it seemed the whole machine would be clumsy and defective and would cost more time to bring to perfection than he felt he should spare from the immediate business of his engine. "After all," he told Anne, "this post chaise business is a luxury. I am more concerned with the necessities of industry."

FIFTEEN

There was definite demand for pumping engines, but with the constant bickering about prices there was very little money coming in. The understanding with the mine owners had been that they would pay the firm the cost of the fuel saved by the new engine. This had seemed satisfactory at the time, but as there was no way of checking on precisely how much fuel was used, and as the mine owners proved to have conveniently faulty memories, the company receipts fell off to almost nothing. Something must be done.

If, Watt figured, he could invent a way of checking the number of strokes made by each engine in a given length of time, he could keep tab on the consumption of fuel.

As usual an idea meant an experiment, and before six months had passed he came up with a piece of clockwork that solved his problem. This consisted of a pendulum worked by a spring and a train of wheels moved by an escapement regulated in the pendulum. These wheels

158

moved a set of dials, similar to a watch face. Each dial—
and there were eight—was differently graduated from
tens, hundreds and thousands and so on, up to an amount
that would count the strokes of an engine going constantly for a year. The pendulum was attached to the
beam of the engine in such a way that the escapement
wheel was turned one tooth for each complete stroke of
the piston. The "counter," as he called it, was enclosed in
a box to which only he, Boulton or Murdock had the key.
No longer would the uncertain minds of the mine owners
estimate the amount of fuel saved. It was now in plain
sight for all to see.

Back to his engine again, Watt tackled a problem that
had troubled him from the start. Originally, when the
beam was used merely to pull the piston up, chains had
been sufficient. Then when he devised the double-acting
engine he had to use solid iron rods that would push as
well as pull. The fundamental fault here was that the
arm of the beam by its very nature moved in an arc; that
is, with a circular motion. The result of this was that the
piston could not work precisely when vertical but was
pulled slightly off center with every stroke. If, then, he
reasoned, he could secure the perpendicular motion by
motions turning on curves, he would have his answer.
The piston would move free of any friction.

For six months he worked on the idea. Then he came
up with what he told Mr. Boulton was a contrivance of
which he was prouder of than any invention he had ever
made. By means of jointed links he turned the circular
motions into a perpendicular one. The piston moved

silently in a smooth up-and-down line with no veering to right or left. He would, he decided, use this in the Albion Mills engines.

The world was beginning to notice James Watt. In 1784 he was made a fellow of the Royal Society of Edinburgh, and the following year he was equally honored by the London Society. It was now James Watt, F.R.S.

The outlook was bright. In 1786 the Albion Mills plant was opened. His engines were, of course, the heart of the plant. They were double-acting and equipped with his latest inventions, the sun and planet rotary mechanism and the governors. This last was a method of regulating the passage of steam between the boiler and the cylinder. It consisted of two balls fixed on the ends of arms connected to the engine by a movable ratchet. As they spun, the centrifugal force would move the ratchet up or down, thus opening or closing the steam valve.

The mill became the talk of England. Thomas Jefferson, who was United States Ambassador to France, came to England to help negotiate for a trade treaty the year the Albion Mills opened, and he wrote home that he had seen an extraordinary grist mill driven, not by water power, but by a steam engine that consumed a hundred bushels of coal a day. Machinery formerly made of wood was now carefully made of cast iron. Corn was ground at the rate of three thousand bushels in twenty-four hours. Bread could be supplied to one hundred and fifty thousand people a year. The grist mill was definitely a success. The lords and ladies of London flocked to see it, which irritated Watt, who felt the idle rich were dramatizing it as a circus.

Then opposition developed. The owners of small wind and water mills saw their future endangered. The complicated monsters that turned the huge grindstones became to them the advance guard of an approaching enemy. They had already moved from the cottage baking ovens to organized flour mills, and to this change they had become accustomed. There was still much individual handwork, and they were satisfied. As word of the success at the Albion Mills spread, hatred and jealousy spread with it.

In the early morning of March 3, 1791, near the end of Blackfriars Bridge in Southmark, everything was quiet. The river Thames was at extreme low tide with sewer openings shamelessly exposed. A few vessels lay quietly at anchor, waiting for the tide to rise. Sleeping beggars were snoring peacefully along the river wall, and the watch had just called its two o'clock "All's Well."

Suddenly many of the windows of the Albion Mills lighted up with a flickering glow. The watch saw it and called "Fire." The glow spread to other windows; there was a crackling of glass, and the glow became a rolling mass of flame. Hand-pumping waters carts were drawn up, but it was found that the handle of the main pump line to the river had been jammed. Attempts were made to pump water from the Thames, but the tide was low and the hand pumps quite inadequate. Throwing water on the flames by a bucket brigade was completely useless, and the Albion Mills crumbled into a heap of smoking debris.

There was no doubt that the fire was deliberate. The jamming of the main pump and the choice of the time of low tide made this only too certain. To Watt it was inconceivable. Cries of monopoly and special privilege were ridiculous. In the five years of its existence the mill had greatly reduced the cost of bread to the very men who burnt it down, and had given work to hundreds of men and women. The fact remained, however, that it was gone, and he, his partner and all the investors faced a loss of ten thousand pounds.

As if the imitators, the arrogant miners, the rising debts and the burning of the Albion Mills were not enough, the French Revolution suddenly became a part of Watt's troubles. The Bastille, the dreary French prison for political prisoners, had fallen in 1789. Joseph Priestley and many of his friends applauded the act publicly, and were accused of being antiroyalist and even antichurch. Two years after the fall of the Bastille, on the night of July 14, 1791, a mob took over Birmingham, burnt many churches and houses, including Priestley's, and forced him to flee to London.

Both Boulton and Watt were personal friends of Joseph Priestley's and fellow members of the Lunar Society. The mob was obviously "anti" philosopher and "anti" any friends of those they stupidly hated. The partners had visions of the destruction of the Soho plant. The nights of July 14th and 15th were filled with terror and suspense. They packed up much that was portable, and took what precautions they could to protect the machinery. Luckily for the future of the steam engine, most of the so-called "antiroyalists" lived at the opposite end of Birmingham, and no harm came to the factory.

This was a company affair, but Watt had a much more personal stake in the French Revolution. His son James, now in his twentieth-fifth year, had been living in France with a Mr. Thomas Cooper. He had become so imbued with the spirit of liberty that at the fall of the Bastille, he became a member of the Jacobin party, an ultra republican group striving to limit the powers of Louis XVI. Young James spoke his mind quite freely, took part in demonstrations and at one point intervened in a duel between the two great party leaders, Danton and Robespierre. He was soundly denounced in the House of Commons by Edmund Burke who had already made violent speeches against the elder Watt in the matter of patents.

Watt knew that young James was inspired by the natural enthusiasm of youth, and that he would modify his sentiments as he grew older. His great fear was that he would not live to grow older, but would succumb to the capriciousness of revolutionary leaders and die under the guillotine. He urged him to return, but up to the moment there was no indication that he would. Time alone would tell, and in the meantime Watt had problems and obligations to attend to that required immediate attention.

The production of engines in imitation of Watt's was growing to alarming proportions. One unfortunate aspect of this was that ignorant people did not distinguish between the real and the imitation. When an imitator's engine failed, it was considered another failure for the Watt engine. Boulton was all for bringing the matter to court and suing the impostors, but Watt heartily disliked this sort of thing. He felt it was possible that they could be reasoned with.

He picked one of the worst offenders, a certain Jonathan Hornblower who had once been a mechanic at Soho, and went to see him at his office in Bristol. He was told that Mr. Hornblower was away, but that he should see the principal partner, a Major Tucker who was just then at Bath. Watt followed him there and was told that the elusive major had gone to Melcampton. He took a chaise and went to Melcampton. The major was out hunting and Watt waited. The major arrived and listened to his arguments, saying he would bring the matter to the attention of Mr. Hornblower. Watt knew perfectly well that this meant absolutely nothing, so he returned home and put a notice in the Birmingham paper warning readers to have nothing to do with the Hornblower engine, and reminding Mr. Hornblower and his representatives that they were violating an authentic patent.

The partners were desperate. Watt was approaching sixty and Boulton was still older. The patent had only seven more years to run, after which anyone so inclined could construct an engine along the same lines. The partners felt that they must recoup by legal means some of the staggering losses they had sustained.

They sued three people in particular—Mr. Hornblower, Mr. Bull, who had worked as a stoker in the Soho factory, and a Mr. Maberly. The trials started in 1793 and dragged on for six years, the final verdict being rendered in 1799, one year before the expiration of the patent. The case appeared to rest on three points: 1. Had Mr. Watt invented only an idea or was it a workable manufacture? 2. Were the specifications clear enough so that any proper mechanic could build from them? and 3. Was the patent valid?

Watt had no trouble at all in persuading his friends to act as witnesses. Besides William Murdock, who volunteered his services, there were William Herschel, the astronomer, Jesse Ramsden, the most famous living inventor of astronomical and optical instruments, and John Rennie, the young man who had designed all the machinery for the ill-fated Albion Mills.

After a few days of the trial, Watt was relieved to see that the defendants were unable to get together any such intelligent group of witnesses. One of the opposition's witnesses was an odd fellow by the name of Joseph Bramah. He asked permission to lay before the court a "few remarks," but was cut short by the judge when His Honor saw that these remarks covered ninety-one printed pages. They were later issued to the public, and Watt read with astonishment such statements as "the specifications for the condenser is a very abstruse and ambiguous concern," and for the steam wheel "a complete jumble of incoherent and absurd ideas." As if this were not enough, Mr. Bramah ended by saying, "It must be obvious to everyone, as it has ever been to me, that Mr. Watt has really invented nothing but what would do more mischief than good to the public." If this was all the opposition could produce, Watt felt more confident, left the matter in the hands of his counselor, Mr. Rous, who had so ably defended him in 1775, and turned his mind to other things.

The year was 1793, and young James had come home. The Reign of Terror in France, with its useless shedding of blood, cured him of his passion for any kind of liberty secured through such horror. He was more than ready to accept his father's offer of partnership in the factory. Watt was, of course, delighted to have him back in England, but a little fearful lest he might be seized by an overzealous government as a traitor to the King. Apparently young James's revolutionary enthusiasm had not reached the ears of George III, or perhaps the King, knowing the elder Watt personally since his visit to the Whitehead brewery, decided to overlook the matter. At all events nothing happened, and James, Jr. became, with his young brother Gregory, aged sixteen, part owner of the Boulton and Watt Factory, known now as Boulton, Watt and Sons. The third son in the partnership was young Matthew Robinson Boulton.

Here was a dream come true. Watt had always hoped that his sons would become part of the firm. If the trial should turn out favorably, and all things pointed to that result, he could put aside responsibility. His engine was a fact, and he could spend the rest of his days peacefully after all the struggles he had gone through. The younger generation would be in charge.

But Fate was still playing with James Watt. Jessie had never been strong, and in spite of all the loving care that Anne and Watt gave her, she grew steadily weaker. Only a few days after the beginning of the trial, she died. Then, hardly was the trial over when he received word that his daughter Margaret, who was married to a Mr. Miller of Glasgow, had died suddenly in her thirty-second year. It seemed to Watt that this was a heavy price to pay for his public success. Even his Scottish reliance on the will of God did little to relieve him of the pain of the double loss.

Inspired perhaps by the enthusiasm of the young partners, the firm made two major changes. They enlarged the factory in order to build complete engines rather than only the parts, and they set up a separate foundry, known as the Soho Foundry, about a mile from the main plant. By making and selling the complete engine, the firm was able to avoid all the bickering that had gone on about fees, as well as the prolonged trips for supervising construction that had taken so much of Jamie's time and effort.

Then in 1799, Boulton and Watt's claims were completely vindicated and the legal validity of the letters patent firmly established. Heavy damages and court costs were levied against the defendants. The many other imitators, seeing the result of the trial and fearful of being sued, were easily prevailed upon to give up much of their ill-gotten gains. Watt was generous and did not overpress his advantage. After all, he was at last publicly recognized as the originator of the separate condenser engine with all its variations.

SIXTEEN

THE YEAR 1800 CAME AROUND. GEORGE III, KING OF England, had lost his American colonies to the United States of America; his dream of supreme kingly power had vanished under the powerful rule of his prime minister, William Pitt. On the contrary, James Watt, the other dreamer had seen his dream realized beyond his expectations.

The face of England had changed, and James Watt had changed it. The conditions of life for hundreds of thousands of men and women had been transformed. Country folk were fast becoming units in a national labor force. No longer did the spinning wheel whir or the hand loom rattle back and forth in the majority of humble cottages. Men and women who for generations had made their own woolen clothes and, more lately, their linen and cotton, went to work every morning in factories where such things were turned out by machines —not machines run by water power or the plodding feet

169

of a horse or the uncertain strength of the wind, but machines run by steam.

When the Boulton and Watt patent expired, the number of engines skyrocketed. Those made by the original firm continued to be the best, but much work was done with cheaper, inferior models constructed on the same principles.

Factories could be set up at any convenient place, near a coal field, near a harbor, or near some large city. It was no longer necessary to choose a spot near a stream for water power. In times of drought the factories did not have to close down. The steam engine kept the wheels running at the touch of a man's hand.

Production increased, and one thing led to another. The greater production made necessary greater distribution, and more and better roads and canals were the result. Foreign markets on the Continent and in the United States and the West Indies were opened, and rivers and harbors were deepened to take care of the increased shipping.

In 1801 on the Forth and Clyde Canal a side-wheeler, the *Charlotte Dundas,* achieved eight miles in one hour and twenty minutes with a Boulton and Watt engine. On board was an American artist, Robert Fulton, who had only recently become interested in engineering. He was much impressed by the *Charlotte Dundas* and in 1807, on returning to the United States, built, on the Hudson River, a ship which he named the *Clermont.* Powered by a twenty-four-horsepower Boulton and Watt engine, the *Clermont* made a successful trip of one hundred and fifty miles from New York to Albany.

The success of the new industrialists, the men owning the various factories, inspired others to do the same. These men had to find money to finance such ventures, and banks sprang up in large numbers. Where the factories were established distant from large cities, towns grew up, and the workers lived here rather than in their distant cottages. The population became divided into townspeople and country folk.

The new steam machines affected every facet of English life. They created a power equal to the work of four hundred million men. They drained mines, blew furnaces, rolled and hammered metal, threshed and ground corn, sawed timber, printed books and drove countless looms and spindles. The tremendously increased production of woolen and cotton goods, especially the latter, made it possible for the average man and woman to have more frequent changes of clothes and consequently, healthier bodies. The removal of the spinning wheels and looms from the small cottages to the factories gave healthier living space for country families. As a result, there was less mortality and a rise in population.

Watt watched all these changes. He saw new roads connecting the various manufacturing centers with each other and with the canals and seaports. A young man named John MacAdam was urging a new method of building them with crushed rock, and Watt remembered how he had ridden horseback over narrow, rutted roads, risking attack by highwaymen. He remembered how he had surveyed routes for the early canals, had built bridges and slashed hillsides. The future would be in younger hands but he, James Watt, had started it all on that Sunday morning in 1765.

He had good reason to be happy and contented. Some years before the end of the century, he and Anne had purchased an estate at Heathfield, near Soho, looking to his old age. He and Boulton had originally agreed that the expiration of the patent would mark the end of their partnership, which was why they put their young sons in the firm before that time. At sixty-four, Watt looked forward to a life free of business worries, his primary ambition in life satisfied. He established a workshop in the attic of his house where he could gather together all his books, tools, plans and specifications, and work on any new ideas that occurred to him. "Without a hobby horse, what is life?" was a favorite saying of his, and his workshop was the place to ride his hobby horse, his "holy of holies."

His family had been tragically reduced. His father, his last family link with Glasgow, had died in 1782, and his responsibilities now were Anne, Jemmy and Gregory. Jemmy was doing remarkably well at the factory, working with great enthusiasm and originality. In 1817, he purchased a ship, the *Caledonia*, which had been laid up for two years because her engine would not work. He installed two new engines of fourteen horsepower each, built at Soho, and set off from Margate for Holland where he arrived a little over twenty-four hours later, having run under steam at an average rate of seven and a half knots an hour. This being the first time that a steam vessel had ever crossed the English Channel, the event caused a sensation on the Continent and in England.

Young Gregory proved to be brilliant as a student at Glasgow College. Handsome and popular, he had won the majority of the prizes at graduation in both literature and science. When he found himself made a partner in the Soho business, he was not happy about it. He had his father's dislike of office work even as he had his love of anything requiring imagination and experimentation. Jemmy sensed this and made it possible for Gregory to spend most of his time away from the factory while still maintaining his rights as a partner.

Then, hardly had he joined the firm than he developed definite signs of lung trouble. Watt sent him to the south of England where he improved enough to take a trip through Europe. At home, finally, in Birmingham, he delighted in assisting his father in chemical experiments, even reading a paper before the Royal Society on fictitious air, a mixture that Watt hoped might help Gregory.

What happened then followed the tragic pattern that had been Watt's family life. Gregory had fits of coughing that racked his body so that he could hardly breathe. His parents took him to Bath and Exeter where he improved very slightly, but soon his condition became worse and in 1804 he died and was buried in the cathedral at Exeter.

Watt was heartbroken and wrote to Matthew Boulton: "One stimulus to exertion is taken away and, somehow or other, I have lost my relish for my usual occupation."

It was as though God were visiting the tribulations of Job on James Watt. Just before Gregory's death, his old friend Dr. Darwin and the good Dr. Priestley had died, and shortly after Gregory's funeral Watt learned of the deaths of John Robison and his old partner, Matthew Boulton.

By this time he felt he should be used to disappointment, trials and loss of family and friends. At the age of seventy-three, he braced himself. He still had much to be thankful for. His thirst for knowledge was as keen as ever even though his fundamental goal had been reached. With his mind free of business worries, his headaches became less frequent and he was able to work sometimes for days at a time in his workshop under the eaves.

Anne was a very particular housekeeper. One speck of dirt was to her one too many, and since it was impossible for Watt to carry on his experiments without some dirt, the boundary between the attic and the rest of the house became a very definite and impenetrable barrier. He even occasionally cooked his noon meal there to avoid the delay in washing and changing his leather apron and work clothes.

He was often asked to put his mind on various industrial problems, to help perfect some intricate piece of machinery or repair some failure. He consistently said "no." He was through with that sort of thing. His life now was his own.

Then in 1811, the Glasgow Waterworks Company

found itself in a dilemma. At great expense the company erected a building on the banks of the Clyde. Scarcely was the construction finished when a spring of beautiful fresh water was found directly opposite on the other bank. Quite naturally, they constructed a pipe line to it, and anticipated no trouble. Nature had other plans; the rigid pipe line, under the changing shape of the river bottom, bent and broke to the point of uselessness. The owners appealed to the Glasgow boy in Birmingham.

Anything out of the ordinary intrigued him and, breaking his rule, Watt agreed to give the matter some thought. He knew very well what the underwater problems were, having as a young man worked on the Clyde River. One night at dinner he was eating a lobster, one of his favorite dishes. As he picked up the tail to dig out the meat, he had a sudden thought. Why not build the Glasgow pipe line on the principle of a lobster's tail?

No sooner thought of than tried. The next year the Glasgow Waterworks Company was pumping the clear, spring water through a thousand feet of lobster-tail pipe, two feet in diameter. Watt refused to take any pay. He was, he said, glad to be of help to his old home town. The company, however, though grateful for this offer, would have none of it, and presented him with valuable silver plate worth over one hundred guineas. He received it in a modest speech, adding, "It is a great thing to find out what will *not* do; it leads to finding out what *will* do."

He was urged constantly to take part in public affairs, being once chosen sheriff, or chief executive officer of his shire or county. With some difficulty he persuaded the authorities that he was far too old to assume any such obligations, and his name was reluctantly withdrawn. His greatest outdoor joy was to walk the mile or so to the Soho plant and look with admiration and pride on the work being done by his son and the son of his old partner, Matthew Boulton. He made frequent trips around England and his beloved Scotland. On one visit to London he was invited to Windsor Castle where he renewed his acquaintance with George III. But as the years passed he spent more time in his garret workshop. He worked in chemistry and optics, even trying to solve the current problem of reproducing a picture on a sensitive surface by the light through a lens, but his real love was his statue-copying machine.

He had long given thought to such an instrument. On his visits to the Continent he had seen and admired many of the world's great sculptures. He had always wished for reproductions for his own home. He was quite proud of the small figures he reproduced, and spoke of them as the work of a young artist entering his eighty-third year.

Fundamentally, the machine consisted of a cutting tool and a guide point so joined that when the guide point, which was blunt, passed over the surface of the statue or medal to be copied, the cutting tool would carve out the copy. As he had done with his steam engine, he constantly made improvements.

In the late summer of 1819 he was starting work on an iron frame for his machine to replace the crude wood which had satisfied him while he was perfecting the cutting tools. It was hot under the eaves and the iron bar in the lathe was not turning to his satisfaction. He stopped the treadle and attempted to adjust the bar properly. His eyes blurred when he tried to match the center of the bar to the guide point on the lathe. When he sat down to rest, he began to cough.

Anne heard him and came running up the stairs.

"Jamie—ye've done enough today. Come and lie down." She helped him to his feet and took off his leather apron. The coughing subsided for a moment, and Watt stood meekly holding fast to Anne. He suddenly had a feeling that he was leaving the attic for the last time, and his eyes hungrily took in all the details. There were models of governors and the parallel motion gear of which he had been so proud—a reflecting mirror, a crude camera with the lens mounted on pasteboard, busts, medallions and figures waiting to be copied, and shelves full of things from the past, kept out of pure sentiment.

Annie led him to the door. As he went out he caught sight of Gregory's hair trunk which held his dead son's books and papers, and his eyes filled with tears.

For days, Watt lay in bed. The cough seemed less severe, but the doctor forbade him to move. He was cheered by visits from Jemmy, and a constant stream of friends, carefully ushered in and out by Anne lest he get overtired. On August 19th, he was chatting with a group around his bed when his headache suddenly became almost unbearable. He grasped Anne's hand and looked at each familiar face. "I thank you for your friendship," he said with a smile. "I feel that I have come to my last illness." The smile faded and James Watt's eyes closed forever.

Five years after James Watt's death, a huge statue in Carrara marble by the famous sculptor Sir Francis Chantrey was voted placed in Westminster Abbey. The city, which fifty-nine years before had refused him employment, now recognized him as a national hero. Subscriptions poured in from men and women of all walks of life. King George donated five hundred pounds. Henry, Lord Brougham, a distinguished member of Parliament, expressed the sentiment of all England in the following inscription:

NOT TO PERPETUATE A NAME

WHICH MUST ENDURE WHILE THE PEACEFUL ARTS FLOURISH

BUT TO SHEW

THAT MANKIND HAVE LEARNT TO HONOR THOSE

WHO BEST DESERVE THEIR GRATITUDE

THE KING

HIS MINISTERS AND MANY OF THE NOBLES

AND COMMONERS OF THE REALM

RAISED THIS MONUMENT TO

JAMES WATT

WHO DIRECTING THE FORCE OF AN ORIGINAL GENIUS

EARLY EXERCISED IN PHILOSOPHICAL RESEARCH

TO THE IMPROVEMENT OF

THE STEAM ENGINE

ENLARGED THE RESOURCES OF HIS COUNTRY

INCREASED THE POWER OF MAN

AND ROSE TO AN EMINENT PLACE
AMONG THE MOST ILLUSTRIOUS FOLLOWERS OF SCIENCE
AND THE REAL BENEFACTORS OF THE WORLD
BORN AT GREENOCK MDCCXXXVI
DIED AT HEATHFIELD IN STAFFORDSHIRE MDCCCXIX

BIBLIOGRAPHY

Allan, Douglas A. *James Watt: A Memory.* Edinburgh, 1955.

Arago, M. *Historical Eloge of James Watt.* London: John Murray, 1839.

Brougham, Lord. *Lives of Men of Letters and Science.* Philadelphia: Carey & Hart, 1845.

Carnegie, Andrew. *James Watt.* New York: Doubleday, Page & Co., 1905.

Cormack, J. D. *In the Days of Watt.* Greenock Philosophical Society, 1915.

Dickinson, Henry W. *James Watt, Craftsman and Engineer.* Cambridge: University Press, 1936.

Dickinson, Henry W. and Jenkins, R. *James Watt and His Steam Engine.* Oxford, Clarendon Press, 1927.

Gale, Walter R. U. *Boulton & Watt and the Soho Undertakings.* Birmingham Museum, 1952.

Grant, John W. *Watt and the Steam Age.* London: St. Bride's Press, 1917.

Hart, Ivor Blashka. *James Watt and the History of Steam Power.* New York: H. Schuman, 1949.

Lang, G. *Great Men of Scotland.* London: Bodley Head, 1957.

Marshall, T. H. *James Watt*. London: L. Parsons, 1925.

Muirhead, James Patrick. *Life of James Watt*. London: J. Murray, 1858.

———— *Origin and Progress of the Mechanical Inventions of James Watt*. London: J. Murray, 1954.

Oliver, Peter. *Saints of Chaos*. New York: W. F. Payson, 1934.

Pagan, Anna M. *James Watt and the Pioneer Inventions*. London: Blackie & Son Ltd., 1928.

Parkman, Mary R. *Conquests of Invention*. New York: The Century Co., 1921.

Preece, William Henry. *Watt and the Measurement of Power*. London: W. Clowes & Son, 1897.

Russell, Phillips. *Harvesters*. New York: Brentano, 1932.

Smiles, Samuel. *Lives of Boulton and Watt*. London: J. Murray, 1868.

INDEX

183

About the Author

WILLIAM D. CRANE was born in
New York City, attended St. Mark's
and Harvard where he was editor of
the *Harvard Advocate*. His premedical
study was interrupted by World War I,
and it was completely abandoned because of ill health. He taught English
at the California Institute of Technol-
ogy, and then opened his own school.
Since his retirement he has published
children's plays, articles on education
and theatre and biographies for young
people.